am I
being kind

Hay House Titles of Related Interest

YOU CAN HEAL YOUR LIFE, the movie,
starring Louise L. Hay & Friends
(available as a 1-DVD program and
an expanded 2-DVD set)
Watch the trailer at: **www.LouiseHayMovie.com**

THE SHIFT, the movie,
starring Dr. Wayne W. Dyer
(available as a 1-DVD program
and an expanded 2-DVD set)
Watch the trailer at: **www.DyerMovie.com**

• • •

*ALL YOU EVER WANTED TO KNOW FROM HIS
HOLINESS THE DALAI LAMA ON HAPPINESS,
LIFE, LIVING, AND MUCH MORE,*
conversations with Rajiv Mehrotra

*A COURSE IN WEIGHT LOSS: 21 Spiritual
Lessons for Surrendering Your Weight Forever,*
by Marianne Williamson

*EXCUSES BEGONE! How to Change Lifelong,
Self-Defeating Thinking Habits,* by Dr. Wayne W. Dyer

*HEALING YOUR FAMILY HISTORY:
5 Steps to Break Free of Destructive Patterns,*
by Rebecca Linder Hintze

Praise for *am I being kind*

"Michael Chase lives and breathes kindness, enthusiasm, and humor. His background, which reminds me of a Stephen King novel, provides living proof that his brand of kindness works miracles. Be kind to yourself. Read this book."

— **Christiane Northrup, M.D.**, *New York Times* best-selling author of *Women's Bodies, Women's Wisdom* and *The Secret Pleasures of Menopause*

"Michael, I read your book yesterday in one sitting because I couldn't put it down. One word: Masterpiece! Thank you, and bravo, my friend."

— **Patrick Combs,** best-selling author of *Major in Success* and founder of **GoodThink.com**

"As we try and navigate ourselves through increasingly hectic and distracted lives, when quiet, simple moments seem rare, **am I being kind** offers us a fresh perspective, allowing us to pause and remember what is truly important in this life: kindness toward ourselves and others. Thank you, Michael!"

— **Lisa Barstow,** author of *Don't Go Back to Sleep, a memoir*

*"So many of us are seeking the answer to 'Why am I here?' We are all blessed that Michael J. Chase has found his own answer—to be 'The Kindness Guy.' Through this priceless work, Michael starts a service-based movement to change our world for the better. As a reader, you can't help but want to become one of his foot soldiers; **am I being kind** is our training manual."*

— **Scott Wittig**, founder of **doITgroups.com** and author of *Holy IT!: The Amazing Power of ClarITy*

"Michael's tireless work is essential to the well-being of us all. He lives, writes, and shares so that others can discover the truly life-changing power of kindness. I wholeheartedly know that the world is changing for the better because of him. I look forward to the day when kindness is not such an unexpected surprise—all because of Michael's work."

— **Kris Wittenberg**, founder of **begoodtopeople.com**

*"Michael J. Chase has it right when he calls kindness 'the vehicle for delivering unconditional love' and 'the creative distribution of love.' The simple and universal set of personal choices presented in **am I being kind** can pave the pathway to happiness, for you and those around you."*

— **Dave Berman**, Manifest Positivity Life Coach and Certified Practitioner of NLP

am I
being kind

*how asking one simple question
can change your life . . .
and your world*

MICHAEL J. CHASE

HAY HOUSE, INC.
Carlsbad, California • New York City
London • Sydney • Johannesburg
Vancouver • Hong Kong • New Delhi

Published and distributed in the United States by: Hay House, Inc.: www .hayhouse.com • **Published and distributed in Australia by:** Hay House Australia Pty. Ltd.: www.hayhouse.com.au • **Published and distributed in the United Kingdom by:** Hay House UK, Ltd.: www.hayhouse.co.uk • **Published and distributed in the Republic of South Africa by:** Hay House SA (Pty), Ltd.: www.hayhouse.co.za • **Distributed in Canada by:** Raincoast: www.raincoast .com • **Published in India by:** Hay House Publishers India: www.hayhouse.co.in

Editorial Supervision: Jill Kramer • *Project editor:* Patrick Gabrysiak
Interior design: Riann Bender

Library of Congress Cataloging-in-Publication Data

Chase, Michael J.
  Am I being kind : how asking one simple question can change your life-- and your world / Michael J. Chase. -- 1st ed.
      p. cm.
   ISBN 978-1-4019-3120-9 (tradepaper : alk. paper) 1. Kindness. 2. Chase, Michael J. I. Title.
  BJ1533.K5C44 2011
  177'.7--dc22

                          2010040674

ISBN: 978-1-4019-3120-9
Digital ISBN: 978-1-4019-3121-6

13 12 11 10   4 3 2 1
1st edition, April 2011

Printed in the United States of America

This book is dedicated to my father, James Allen Chase. Although it was difficult to understand our path at times, I now see the perfection and significance in each moment. I love you, Dad. . . .

— Father's Day, June 21, 2009

*"Be kind, for everyone you meet
is fighting a hard battle."*

— PHILO

Contents

PART III: Livingkindness: Kindness as a Way of Life

Introduction

This is a book about *global warming*—not in an environmental sense, but rather a gradual warming of the human heart. For in our family settings, workplaces, schools, and daily social interactions, we have sadly allowed a layer of iciness to form over our planet for far too long. The icebergs of oppression, prejudice, and a variety of daily acts of unkindness are compounding, one on top of another, at such a quickening pace that unless we start the melting process now . . . we may soon be facing another ice age.

Of course, most of us say we want a kinder and more peaceful world—one where we are friendlier, have more patience, are less judgmental, and act in loving and compassionate ways. But many people would also agree that if we're feeling down and uninspired, we find it more difficult to be kind. With all of the pressures of work, finances, relationships, parenting, health issues, and any other stressors, living a kindhearted life isn't always easy. The truth is, those who consistently lack positive emotions in their lives more often than not tend to generate much of the world's unkindness.

World Peace Begins with Inner Peace

My goal in writing *am I being kind* is to help you realize that your own happiness is actually the key to creating a more peaceful and kind world. Inspired by the Dalai Lama's philosophy that "world peace must develop out of inner peace," this book will show you why fulfilling relationships, an inspiring career, and vibrant health are not only necessary for your own well-being, but they also have a positive impact on every single being on the planet. Simply put, when people are authentically joyful and inspired, they are more likely to be kind.

Unfortunately, it took me most of my life to realize this. As someone who was once unhappy in every sense of the word, I can personally verify that misery leads to heartless behavior, and vice versa. For years I experienced failed relationships, financial struggles, poor health, depression, and an endless stream of negative habits. It seemed that no matter how hard I tried, true contentment eluded me as if I were working off karmic debt for crimes that I committed in a past life.

Looking back, I now understand that the reason I couldn't "find myself" was because I'd been searching in all the wrong places. I didn't realize that the answers to everything I ever wanted would be found in the last place I'd thought to look: inside my own heart. There it was, the secret to happiness, beating in my chest all along.

Not only did this awareness dissolve my personal suffering, but it also gave me the profound realization that my life's purpose was the complete opposite of what I'd originally imagined. After all, in our culture we're often indoctrinated at an early age to believe that chasing external conditions such as money, relationships, and material items will bring us fulfillment.

Eventually, I found that true satisfaction simply couldn't be achieved by living in this way. For me, bliss came through opening my heart to the world and rediscovering the essence of who *I* really am— and who *you* really are, too: love and kindness.

am I being kind—What Does It Mean?

Often when I discuss the material in this book, someone asks me about the title—"Why don't you capitalize it?" "Why isn't there a question mark at the end?" The answer is simple: *it came to me that way.* First seen in a morning meditation, this inner mantra floated across the screen in my mind exactly as you see it. (I've often joked that meditation doesn't have spell-check.) For days I considered its meaning and how it may be relevant to everyday life. I just couldn't stop thinking about it. But I finally did get it out of my head . . . and into my heart. And that's where I discovered the true power of this question, just as you will within these pages.

At one point, I thought of the word *kindness* as just a warm and fuzzy way of being nice. I never would have imagined that it could be used as a method for personal and spiritual development. But after devouring hundreds of books, attending inspirational workshops and seminars, meditating, praying, saying affirmations, and absorbing the wisdom of the world's greatest spiritual teachers, I have yet to find anything as profound as adopting kindness as a guiding principle. Maybe that's because, unlike some systems that encourage only personal growth, this method not only changes your life . . . but it also changes the lives of others.

Perhaps the true spirit of *am I being kind* is to demonstrate that no matter where you are right now, or how much you've been through in the past, you can always begin again. I have found that many people believe it's too late or even impossible to alter their path and make a different decision. *This is simply not true.* In writing this book, it is my intention to give you a newfound sense of hope, while also revealing the life-changing power of kindness. Having personally lived this philosophy, I can verify its astonishing results. I'll even go so far as to say that I've seen miracles happen. It doesn't matter what religion you believe in, how old you are, what color your skin is, if you're male or female, or what corner of the earth you live on—kindness is a universal language that *everyone* can speak.

Developing a Kindness Consciousness

The following pages offer a unique program for increasing happiness in your life while creating a better world in the process. Through stories, real-life examples, and valuable tools that you can use every day, *am I being kind* will show you how a lifestyle of kindness can transform negative emotions and unwanted habits into vibrant energy and an inspired existence.

In Part I, I share my personal experiences from my less-than-kind past, which led me to search for an alternative path, have a profound awakening, and write the book you're now holding in your hands.

Part II explains exactly how to develop the skills and perspectives that lead to a fulfilling life. Through a process that I call Seven Choices, you'll be offered two options in seven different areas. One leads to personal success and kinder living, while the other ensures a pathway of disappointment and conflict. Each choice is modeled after my own experiences, as well as studies of the happiest people in the world.

The last section, Part III, is the pinnacle of *am I being kind.* Here you'll be presented with five principles called the 5 Keys to Kindness. You'll also be given descriptions of the elements that compose a kind heart, along with detailed examples of each one in action. If you embrace these principles each day, they'll bring you more joy and inner freedom than anything you've ever known.

How to Get the Most from This Book

Receiving the greatest benefit from this book requires *applying* its principles consciously. As I mentioned earlier, I wrote it based on the idea that a blissful life leads to a kinder life . . . and ultimately a better world. Simply stated, *to make the greatest difference in the world, you must first love who you are.* The techniques presented in *am I being kind* are designed to show you what's necessary to do exactly that. Here's how you can make this material work best for you:

First, you might want to get a notebook or journal to record your responses to exercises and questions in Parts II and III, as well as any insights and inspirations that come to you as you read. And second, do take the time that's necessary to integrate the concepts, absorb the stories, and consider what they all mean to you. You'll gain the most from this book by reading it slowly.

As you complete the Seven Choices in Part II, you'll be challenged to shift old beliefs into a new, heart-centered perspective by asking yourself, "am I being kind?" in each area. It's vital that you work through these choices sequentially, *even if some are not an issue for you now.* These exercises will build your "heart muscle" and awareness so you can support yourself and others in challenging situations. At the end of each of these chapters, you'll find personal contracts to sign, which confirm that you're agreeing to this new way of living. It's highly encouraged that you complete each one; while doing so may seem simple, the act of signing your name actually has tremendous power.

• • •

So let's begin! A whole new journey, a whole new life, and a whole new world await you. Whether you're just starting on your path of self-discovery, or you're an experienced traveler, I know there's something here that's *just for you*. It may be a series of chapters or perhaps one eye-opening sentence, but I promise you this: if you're willing to quiet your mind and fully open your heart, your universe will never look the same.

Kindness. It almost seems too simple. Could changing your life really be that easy?

As a matter of fact . . . yes, it is.

• • • • • •

part i

On the Road to Kindness

Chapter 1

The Art of Unkindness

As I pushed my way to the front door, the nause-ating smell of cigarettes, combined with the sounds of obnoxious drunks, car horns, and people yelling, made me wonder why I'd ever spent time in these places to begin with. I despised the whole bar scene and had always promised myself I'd never be a part of it. Nevertheless, I had just spent the past three hours nursing the same drink, hoping that no one would notice my expression of disgust. To be honest, I hated the taste of beer, or any alcohol for that matter.

It was just before midnight, and Halloween was almost over. I looked like a complete freak, but so did everyone else in the bar. I was dressed from head to toe in black, my face was frosted with white makeup, and there were hints of red blood from fake bullet wounds across my neck and chest. Deep black circles painted around my eyes made me look like the raccoon from hell, and the final touch was a plastic .357 Magnum revolver that I'd purchased earlier from a toy store. Loosely tucked into my belt, the gun—with its black handle and chrome barrel—looked very realistic and caused people to look down whenever I glared their way. It appeared as if I'd just been in a bloody fight with God knows who or what, but the truth was, the only thing I was battling on this night was myself.

Earlier that day, without anyone knowing my intentions, I'd begun the process of saying good-bye to family, friends, and even people I hadn't seen in years. Surprisingly, it was quite easy to say my secret farewells. And as the day wore on, an unexpected sense of peace actually began to settle over me.

Even in the moment that I saw my three-year-old son, Alex, I felt that my plan for this day was completely right. Perhaps it was because I honestly felt that his life would be better off without my energy of sadness surrounding his innocent little world, but most of my reasoning for what I was about to do was purely selfish. I was just so tired of the misery that followed me around. I saw no light at the end of the tunnel and, frankly, no longer believed that happiness even existed. I'd been stuck in this poor excuse for a life for 24 years now, and I'd finally had enough.

• • •

When I eventually made it to the sidewalk outside the bar, I only had one thing on my mind: finding my cousin Tammi. She had just spent the past three hours with me, and although she didn't know it, she was to be my final hug. Tammi was one of the few highlights in my life. She was not only my cousin, she was like a best friend and big sister rolled into one. Despite my less-than-kind qualities, her kindness toward me was always a ray of light. For some reason, she always made time for me and showed nothing but love and support for my messed-up life.

Hugging her on this night was not so much a good-bye as it was a thank-you. I desperately wanted to tell her that I loved her, but I thought she might see this as a red flag. Not wanting to give her any reason to worry, I put my arms around her, smiled, and simply said, "Talk to ya soon," as we each turned and began walking in different directions. Just out of earshot, I decided to say it anyway: "Love you."

Where I lived was only a five-minute drive from the bar, but I decided to take a longer route home. Rather than walking to my car, I began a slow-paced journey down Main Street. I knew what was waiting for me at my apartment, but I needed the extra time to think about the note I was going to write. I had a general idea of what I would say, but I wanted to make it very clear that this was *my* choice. Sure, I had my reasons, such as a broken heart from another failed relationship, no real purpose in life, and the childhood from hell, but the last thing I intended to do was place blame on anyone else for my actions on this night. *Besides,* I thought, *I really don't have the energy to blast my father for all of my misery right now.*

And that was all it took. Revisiting the past and thinking about my father was like turning on a furnace inside of me. With each thought of him, fiery anger would build within me. As I continued my trek up the street, it wasn't long before obscenities began flowing under my breath, as I was now thinking, *Yes, it is his fault.*

My father was perhaps my greatest teacher in life. Unfortunately, his expertise consisted of unkindness and a white-hot temper, which often produced storms that would usually find my mom and me in their path. His furious outbursts were regular occurrences and could be triggered by dirt on the floor, a dusty coffee table, excess noise, or even a plate of food that wasn't warmed to the proper temperature.

The reasons for Dad's behavior didn't really matter. What did matter was that we had a safe place to hide until he calmed down.

Still making my way toward home, I recalled how my father's strength almost seemed superhuman to me as a kid. Although he was a small man, he could use his viselike grip to hurl me around, pinning me to a wall or my bedroom ceiling as if gravity temporarily didn't exist. I was absolutely terrified of him, and each day began with the fear of his unpredictable moods and unkind words. I'm not sure who came up with the saying "Sticks and stones may break my bones, but words can never hurt me," but in my experience, this wasn't true at all. Cruel words can remain tattooed on a person's soul for a lifetime.

A Vicious Cycle

As gifted as my father was at the art of unkindness, he had learned his skills from a true master: our next-door neighbor, my grandfather. He was a large, intimidating man who often reeked of body odor and booze, and the closest thing to evil I'd ever seen. His mental and physical acts of violence were the stuff found in horror movies. Firing a shotgun at his children, attempting to burn down the house, holding my grandmother at gunpoint, and kicking the family dog to death provide only a small glimpse of his insanity. He loved his guns and the wicked use of fire. Burning our belongings was a coldhearted hobby of his, and no items were safe. Once, after my favorite toys were left in his yard, they were quickly gathered up, placed in a metal barrel, doused with gasoline, and . . . well, you get the picture.

My grandfather's cruel behavior became the foundation for all of my father's personal anguish, and (lucky me) his parenting skills as well. But this was tradition, after all. Beginning with my not-so-great-grandfather, the art of unkindness would be passed on to my grandfather, to my father, and then to me, ensuring that a "World's Greatest Dad" T-shirt would never hang in a Chase family closet. Each son's feelings of resentment toward his own father simply put a bull's-eye on the back of generations to come, as a wounded child would grow into an angry teen, and eventually an adult filled with depression and searing bitterness.

It was during my early 20s when my own mental war began to rage. A constant battle between self-loathing and blame felt like grenades going off in my head. Jagged pieces of shrapnel in the form of hatred toward my father peppered my mind whenever I thought about my childhood. And like so many soldiers who come back from war, I started to become a prisoner to nightmares and, especially, resentment for my stolen youth.

Fortunately, when I became a father at 21, I was able to keep most of this internal turmoil under control through suppression. I'd promised myself never to express my pain around Alex or allow him to be a part of our family history. Each day I worked at finding new ways to keep my negative emotions inside, while showering him with love and affection. What I felt for my little boy was indescribable. He was the only thing on this earth that truly made me happy, and I was determined to do whatever it took so that he would never become anything like my father or me.

The problem was, however, that I was no longer living with him. I had tried for years to make things work with his mother, but she and I were simply not meant to be together. While being separated from her had actually been quite easy, not living with Alex was killing me. As a weekend dad, Monday through Friday became incredibly lonely and caused me a tremendous amount of pain. I wished I could be with him so much. I missed our special morning time before I left for work. I missed watching cartoons with him. I even missed the messy piles of stuffed animals, Matchbox cars, and plastic action figures scattered across the living-room floor. My daily prayer was: "God, please, let us be together again. Please let Alex live with me and not his mother."

I tried to fill this void with dating and working on a career as a professional photographer, but as time went on, it just didn't get any easier. Each relationship failed within weeks, and my job was going nowhere fast. It wasn't long before deep depression and the resentment I harbored toward my father finally came to a head . . . and I was sure that my destiny was to follow in his footsteps. Night after night, I sat alone in a run-down attic apartment wondering why I should go on. I never told anyone about these thoughts, for fear that I wouldn't be allowed to see my son anymore. But it got to a point where I was just so tired of hurting all the time. I felt like a time bomb waiting to go off, and I'd finally convinced myself on that Halloween morning that life was no longer worth living. I hated my life. I hated my father. And I especially hated myself.

The Bad Guy

It was now past midnight, and instead of going to my apartment, I'd circled the downtown area at least once. Most of the people who had lingered outside of the bar had either gone home or made their way to the town's Halloween hot spot: Stephen King's mansion. Despite being shielded by iron gates and gargoyles, his fortress attracted a loitering crowd of kids and adults alike every October 31. Personally, I couldn't have cared less whether Stephen King was greeting trick-or-treaters or not. No fistful of a celebrity's candy corn was going to change what was going on inside my head.

Still drenched in self-pity while fuming about my father, I just wanted this night to be over. Completely exhausted and even more depressed by this point, I remember thinking, *Forget the note; I've said my good-byes.*

Seconds later, just as I'd turned in the direction of my apartment, my grim mood was interrupted by the sound of a roaring engine and flashes of blue light coming down Main Street. I'd seen this scene a hundred times before during my obsession with any action flick starring Bruce Willis or Arnold Schwarzenegger, but as the squad car continued to accelerate down the hill, it soon became evident that this was no movie. Numerous people were now pointing in my direction, and I heard shouts of "He's got a gun!" coming from across the street. *Who?* I thought. *And why are they pointing at me?* Looking down, I finally noticed the toy gun clenched in my pasty white fist. Without realizing it, I'd made my .357 Magnum a bit too public during my walk home. Then it all became quite clear: if this was a scene from a movie, I was definitely the bad guy.

As I turned toward the police car, which was now speeding in my direction, the angry growl of its engine was quickly followed by the sound of four screeching tires and the smell of burning rubber. As the cruiser abruptly parked in the middle of Main Street and an officer emerged, the shouts of "He's got a gun" were replaced by a deep voice from behind the car door instructing me to "Put the gun down! Put it down *now!*" With one hand on his gun (which seemed much more realistic than mine), the police officer gave his second warning, only this time with a softer voice: "Son, please put the gun down."

After hearing his second command, I remember that it became unusually quiet. All of the external noise around me seemed to disappear, leaving an eerie silence that perhaps accompanies all moments before death. The crowd across the street, the traffic, and the purr of the police car's motor were replaced by my ever-increasing heartbeat and one reckless thought: *Point your gun at him. Make him shoot you. This is a much cooler way to go.* The whole plan I had waiting for me back at the apartment now seemed so lame in comparison. *This is something that people will remember.*

The officer then spoke again, repeating his authoritative command. "Son, no one needs to get hurt; please just put the gun down." His eyes that were still glaring through me were intense, yet at the same time strangely compassionate. Something about him began to make me believe that he cared. Not just cared, but actually cared about *me*.

I started to wonder, *Did I know this guy? Did he know me?* Then something unexpected began to happen. As I looked back at a man who could easily blow a hole in me at any second, I began to feel empathy toward him.

I could now see beyond his uniform and trigger finger that he truly was concerned for my well-being, and the last thing on his mind was hurting me. With each passing second, I started to see this situation through his eyes, thinking that my stupidity was likely causing him a tremendous amount of anxiety.

What a horrible position I've put him in. I also recall contemplating the kind of psychological damage that would be inflicted upon this poor guy if he shot some idiot carrying a toy gun. It would likely haunt him forever.

For the first time all day, I was no longer being selfish. *What if he has a wife and kids?* Seconds later, my son's beautiful little face suddenly began to flash across my mind. The heartbreaking images of him being fatherless made my knees go weak. *How would anyone ever explain this to my little boy?* Then vivid images of Tammi surged through me. I knew this would crush her. After all, she would have been the last person to see me alive.

Making a Different Choice

At one point, a wave of intense emotions washed over me as I flashed back to a promise I'd made to my mother years before. The memory was of me as a young boy crying with her on my bedroom floor. My distress was a response to one of my father's angry outbursts. What had caused it on that particular day is unclear now, but I'm sure that his reaction was the same old thing—enraged screaming and violent rearranging of the furniture, followed by a typical but

14

ineffective apology. And although I'd seen this pattern more times than I care to imagine, this day was different. For the first time in my life, I did something that my great-grandfather, my grandfather, and my own father were never able to do: I found the courage to make a different choice.

I felt terrified and weak on that particular day, but I didn't let those emotions control me as they had in the past. I knew I was next in line to inherit these destructive qualities, but I also knew that I was the only one who could stop it. This was to be a defining moment in my life. Wiping the tears from my face, I looked at my mother and made her a promise that I was going to somehow find a better way. I was determined to break the chain of drinking, depression, and unspeakable acts of violence. Although I didn't know it at the time, I was about to choose a life of love and kindness over fear and abuse.

As quickly as that memory had appeared, it vanished when I was brought back to my immediate surroundings by an insistent voice: "Son, I'm going to ask you again to please put the gun down." Once again, I was standing in front of the officer whose eyes still expressed compassion but whose stance said, "I will pull the trigger if I have to." At this point, my arm was completely weak and my "weapon" felt like a cinder block. I knew what I had to do. Finally ready to end the drama, my heart opened, my grip loosened, and the ridiculous sound of plastic clinking against the sidewalk broke the silence. My toy gun now lay on the ground as I was being smashed, face-first, into a brick wall.

The imprint of white makeup against the building would surely remain a conversation piece for days to come. But as the officer kicked my feet apart and continued checking my pockets for anything that resembled a real weapon, I remember feeling nothing but peace. I wasn't concerned about potential jail time, or even what others thought of me. It all seemed so insignificant now. I had been given the gift of a second chance, and I knew that there must be a reason for my existence. What that was exactly, I had no idea, but something inside told me that a new chapter in my life was about to begin.

• • •   • • •

Chapter 2

Storms and Epiphanies

Although my life after the Halloween incident wasn't exactly easy, I was slowly beginning to make peace with myself and the world around me. I'll admit that I still had a long way to go, but in the four years that followed, many things began to change. I'd finally met a wonderful girl, convinced her to marry me, and moved from central Maine to southern Maine to pursue my dream of building a successful photography business. And although my son and I were now living 160 miles apart, each Friday I would make the five-hour-round-trip drive so that Alex could be with me until Sunday, when I would take him back to his mother's house. The long hours in the car were tough, but being able to spend weekends with him was worth every mile.

After a couple of years, however, my daily prayers were finally answered. When Alex was eight, he moved in with us full-time, which became my greatest achievement in life. My wife, Cara, quickly took on the role of a loving stepmom, and we officially became a family.

I was 30 years old and things were finally beginning to fall into place. My photography career was taking off, I was gaining more confidence in myself, and my father and I were actually developing a close relationship. Through therapy, medication, and his own will to change, he'd worked very hard at becoming a better person. He was now telling me that he was proud of me and often mailed cards that said "I love you." He even apologized and expressed his regrets for not being the dad he wished he could have been. For the first time in his life, he was opening up his heart to me.

My father was basically a good man who had simply been haunted by the sadistic behavior of my grandfather. I now understood that this was the primary cause of his unkind actions toward me. He didn't hate me. He didn't think I was a bad kid. He just couldn't find a positive way to deal with his emotional pain. Therapy definitely helped, but perhaps the biggest change took place in the early '90s when he became a grandfather.

I have to admit that, in the beginning, it wasn't easy to watch my father spend time with my son. It wasn't because he acted callous or treated him poorly, but rather . . . because he was so loving and kind. I was now seeing qualities in my dad that were rarely evident during my own childhood. He was so sweet, and his newfound patience was miraculous. The affection he gave Alex would sometimes cause my eyes to well up with tears. It was all very bittersweet at first, but over time I finally began to see the grace in their relationship. In addition to my son having a wonderful grandfather, I could now see that this was my father's redemption. Life had given him a second chance, and his grandchildren became a direct path toward authentic joy and a way to let go of past regrets.

This new perspective caused me to forget about my own childhood and instead feel empathy for my father and all that he'd gone through. And even though I'd still occasionally struggle with the past from time to time, I'd finally found a place deep within where I could forgive him. My dad was simply a product of his own childhood environment. We still had some things we needed to work on, but a healthy father-son bond was beginning to form. For the first time in years, life seemed to be finally working for me rather than against me.

Happily married and living in a nice apartment, it was hard to believe that I'd spent a summer living out of a 1978 Cutlass Supreme just ten years prior, often falling asleep to the voices of my most faithful companions—the broadcasters of Red Sox baseball. But those days were long gone. It now appeared that all of my personal dramas and storms had finally passed. My dreams were coming true, and the future looked brighter than ever. An unfamiliar feeling of contentment began to flow into my life and, dare I say, I was actually . . . happy. The universe, however, had other plans. I was completely unaware that the biggest emotional hurricane of my life was on its way. . . .

April 12, 2000

It was just after 11 P.M. when the sound of the doorbell woke us. Bleary-eyed and confused, my wife and I made our way through the apartment, careful not to wake our son from a sound sleep. As we opened the door, a tall, thin police officer stood on our steps. "Mr. Chase?" he said.

Hesitantly, I whispered, "Yes, I'm Michael Chase," hoping that our car had not been another victim of neighborhood teenagers with BB guns.

In a professional tone, but with a hint of sadness in his eyes, he asked, "May I please come in?" His body language told me that something was very wrong, and it had nothing to do with our car.

"Sure," was all I could say as I started to feel waves of anxiety. Ducking his head through the door frame while removing his hat, he politely had us sit down. Just the way he moved sent an overwhelming feeling of dread through me, as I was now certain that I didn't want to hear whatever news he was about to deliver.

As I took a seat on the sofa with my wife close to my side, the officer wasted very little time: "I'm so sorry to tell you this . . . but your father is dead."

Within seconds, my heart was pounding like a jackhammer as tears filled my eyes. In complete shock and disbelief, "How? When?" was all I could get out.

Obviously wanting to finish this difficult assignment as quickly as possible, the officer spoke softly but without any hesitation. "It appears that your father committed suicide sometime yesterday—a self-inflicted gunshot wound to the head. Again, I am truly sorry, Mr. Chase."

It was just too hard to believe. I heard screams of *No, it's not true!* begin in my head. I then closed my eyes, hoping that I would wake up from this horrible dream. After letting several seconds pass, I slowly reopened my eyes, only to see that I was in fact experiencing the reality of my whole world crashing down. Anger and indescribable pain turned soft tears into uncontrollable sobbing and violent shaking that caused my muscles to ache for days . . . and my heart to remain broken for years.

Although he'd made incredible progress, my father simply couldn't escape the demons of his past. For 54 years he battled everything from depression and divorce to regrets as a parent and deep-seated beliefs of worthlessness. Despite the fact my grandfather had passed away in 1986, his voice of ridicule continued to torment my father. All the therapy and antidepression medication in the world simply couldn't close the wounds his own father had created.

• • •

My dad's death became a defining moment for me. Once the initial pain of losing him began to fade, I made a life-altering decision. On a cold, gray day in December 2000, I stood at his grave site and made him a promise that I would not only change my own life, but I'd also make a difference in the lives of others. I had no idea how or when this would happen, but for the first time in 30 years I felt as if I knew what my purpose was.

Over the next several years, I completely immersed myself in the teachings of the world's greatest personal- and spiritual-development gurus. Eckhart Tolle, Dr. Wayne W. Dyer, Ram Dass, and the Dalai Lama became some of my most influential teachers. During this time, my photography career was absolutely thriving, but my main focus had become discovering the secrets to happiness. I was completely obsessed with the science of personal fulfillment—both for myself and with the thought of one day helping others. Through workshops and spending way too much time in the self-help section at the bookstore (the employees there think I'm a total nut), I'd learned hundreds of techniques for living with more joy.

But despite mastering a variety of techniques for managing my emotions, something still seemed to be missing. Although these new ideas had a major impact on the quality of my life, I was still searching for that one universal path that worked for *everyone*.

Whether we're African American, Caucasian, Native American, Asian, Christian, Jewish, Muslim, Buddhist, Hindu, atheist, or an animal with four legs and a tail, I knew there had to be something that benefited all beings, simply because we all want the same thing: *to be happy.*

Coming Out of My Shell

Enlightenment and epiphanies can show up in some pretty strange ways. The Buddha found it under a Bodhi tree, Nelson Mandela in prison, and spiritual guru Ram Dass through psychedelic drugs. Little did I know that my epiphany would arrive in the form of a turtle that was simply trying to cross the road. But this wasn't just any hard-shelled reptile; it was the world's most optimistic turtle. He was tenaciously determined to cross 20 feet of blacktop as cars zoomed by at 55 miles per hour. (Yes, I said "he." Only a *male* would be stubborn enough to think that he could actually make it.) But today was his lucky day. My wife's quick driving reflexes not only ensured that we wouldn't be having turtle soup for dinner that night, but her act of kindness would eventually become the foundation for everything I teach today.

After we avoided running the turtle over by mere inches, we both agreed that we needed to turn around for what seemed like a simple rescue mission. Having found a safe place to park, I quickly hopped out of the car in the hopes of getting to him before any oncoming traffic did. I had no idea that my whole world was about to change.

As I made my way toward the middle of the road, a strange silence fell over the entire scene. There was no wind and no sound of birds singing. Not a single car passed us the entire time we were there. All traffic on the normally busy street had completely stopped. I slowly walked toward the turtle, and I could now see that this creature, which looked like a rock with legs, was making very little progress. The fact that God would create something with four legs that was so slow almost seemed like a cruel joke.

Bending down, I gently placed my fingers underneath him and cradled his body in the palms of my hands. As I rotated his shell, admiring his prehistoric features, his tiny head slowly began to emerge and we were now looking into each other's eyes . . . and that's when it happened. In that moment, something strange yet beautiful began to take place. As I stood there, making eye contact with this little turtle, a wave of pure joy came over me. It was that warm, emotional sensation that we get during life's greatest moments—when we fall in love or during the birth of a child, for example. I honestly had the sensation that my heart was completely opening up while everything else stood still around me. In no way would I have described the experience as Buddha-like enlightenment, but there was no doubt about it—helping this turtle just felt so damn good! But why? After all, it's just a turtle, right? And then it hit me. I finally realized what was happening.

After gently placing my new friend back in the woods, a flood of inspiring thoughts surged through me. I walked back to the car, opened my journal, and wrote eight words that would later prove to be life-changing for me: "kindness creates happiness" and "live a life of kindness."

The simple act of helping my green guru had revealed that a benevolent act was the key to getting out of my analytical mind and into my intuitive heart space. I now understood that any thought, word, or act delivered from the heart had the power to dissolve emotional suffering. It was the answer I'd been looking for. The secret to inner peace and lasting happiness was *kindness*—not random acts of kindness or simply being nice, but rather, kindness as a way of life. I'd already become familiar with the benefits of being kind through studying many Eastern philosophies, but I'd never actually considered it to be a *lifestyle!* And the day was just beginning. . . .

Front-Porch Revelations

Thirty minutes after my mini-epiphany, Cara and I arrived at a country garden show, which was our original destination. After we'd walked around for a few minutes, a gentle-faced man who was probably in his late 60s waved me over to the front porch of his farmhouse for no apparent reason. The entire setting was like a scene out of an old movie—weathered rocking chairs, the smell of cookies baking, and a coon cat that looked as old as the farmhouse itself.

Gesturing toward my wife, the man said, "Let her look around. Come and sit with me." I had no idea what to expect, but as I sank into the large wicker chair beside him, I couldn't help but feel that he was going to say something profound. After all, if a turtle can change my life, why not a wise old farmer? Following a brief hello and a polite introduction, we then sat in silence and let the sunlight warm our faces.

After what seemed like an eternity, he finally spoke. "You know," he began, "I've often thought that the meaning of life is making things a little bit easier for those around us. What do you think?"

I was speechless. It was as if I'd just been hit on the head again with a big karma stick. He went on to tell me his version of "the secrets to life" and how "true happiness can only be found by loving and serving others." Finally he finished with, "Oh, and don't forget, you really gotta love the one you're with . . . yourself." Life was obviously trying to tell me something.

In the weeks after that encounter, the world looked completely different to me. The more I studied and tested my "kindness creates happiness" theory, the more I was blown away by its power. It was the cure to so many of life's ailments: negative emotions such as anger, depression, bitterness, jealousy, and hatred simply couldn't survive when they were confronted by thoughts or acts of kindness.

But there was more. Studies were showing that kindhearted people were receiving amazing benefits, such as fulfilling relationships, a lower divorce rate, a stronger sense of spirituality, relief from anxiety and depression, deep feelings of self-worth, jobs they loved, and even longer lives! In addition to those wonderful "perks," they also experienced *karmic kindness.* By thinking and acting in kinder ways, they were attracting new opportunities and positive events, proving that there are magnetic qualities to our thoughts and actions. It was a no-brainer; kind individuals were happier and healthier, and led more fulfilling lives.

But these new revelations also made me wonder: *If kindness can create happiness, why are there so many unhappy people in the world? What is causing so much suffering?* The answer was so incredibly obvious that I swear I heard the universe say, "Duh!" If kindness creates happiness, then *unkindness creates unhappiness.* It was just that simple; those who are unkind toward others, the environment, and especially themselves, end up being the most miserable people on the planet.

This was a huge wake-up call to self-responsibility. I realized that most of my disappointments occurred simply because I'd been unkind to others and myself. It was now clear that my years of approval seeking and egotistical behavior were the greatest source of my problems. After spending most of my adult life thinking, *What's in it for me?* my new inner guidance became *am I being kind.*

The way I personally applied the meaning of this new mantra was: "Would I want my son to behave in the way I am about to act?" Now, whenever I feel the need to argue with my wife, lash out at a rude employee in the mall, or even shove ten cookies into my mouth (obvious unkindness toward my body), I go within and ask: *am I being kind*. Doing this on a daily basis has become my source of inner and outer peace. It has created many positive changes in me, such as recycling, being more environmentally friendly, and consciously respecting all forms of life. I've even stopped setting out mousetraps in my garage—which isn't a completely popular move at our home.

Another big shift for me was the irresistible urge to perform "spontaneous acts of kindness." Simple things like buying coffee for the person behind me in line and giving money to homeless people on the street just seemed natural. Even the small gesture of letting cars pull ahead of me in traffic would send a blissful surge of energy through my chest. But what became even more exhilarating were the intense feelings of warmth I had toward everyone around me— especially those who were difficult to get along with. Whether there was someone who acted rude in traffic or an inconsiderate person in line at the grocery store, I no longer got angry or offended; I simply wished for his or her happiness. That's when I realized what it truly meant to be *living* kindness.

• • •   • • •

Chapter 3

From Toll House to Hay House

Four months following my turtle epiphany (and with surprisingly little contemplation), I completely shocked everyone around me by announcing that my wife and I were going to close our successful photography business and open something called The Kindness Center. Most people were convinced that I'd completely lost my marbles, and I'll admit there were a few times when I'd wondered if I had, too. Considering that I had absolutely no clue how I'd make this work—and with only a few months' worth of savings in the bank—I guess it did seem a little crazy. But each time doubt or fear crept into my mind, my heart's voice was simply too loud to ignore. I *knew* this was something I was destined to do.

The mission of The Kindness Center was to inspire the world to adopt kindness as a way of life. My vision was to create a teachable system so that people could learn how to make kindness an actual lifestyle—practicing it toward themselves, others, and the earth. I knew in my soul that it was a great concept, but never in my wildest dreams did I expect it to take off so fast.

Within months, I was working with schools, businesses, and a variety of organizations. I also began creating inspirational events based on performing random acts of kindness, which received media coverage all over the world. All of this and more took place despite the fact that we had opened our doors just as our country entered a full-scale recession. How is this possible? Trust me, there are days when I'm still amazed by our rapid accomplishments. But I guess if I really stopped to think about it, I'd tell myself the same thing I teach others during my workshops and events: *anything is truly possible when you listen to your heart.*

When I created The Kindness Center, I knew that kindness was a message that every person could relate to regardless of age, race, or religion. One of my earliest presentations was to an adorable group of about six or seven Girl Scout Daisies. Each one of them possessed the gifts of all great spiritual masters: they were joyful, curious, and simple; but most of all, they lived in the present moment. Watching them was like a meditation in itself. And although I wanted to share this philosophical observation with them (along with the secrets to the universe), I decided goody bags filled with pencils, stickers, and candy might be a better way to keep these tiny gurus happy.

For the hour that I had their attention, I did my best to share the message of kindness in a way that would be easy for them to understand. At times the girls looked excited and eager to learn, while at other moments their expressions flat-out said, "What is this weird guy talking about?"

I'll admit it: simplifying my thoughts on life when speaking to young children or teens is often a challenge for me. After years of feeding my mind with everything from basic psychology and Buddhism to the Law of Attraction, science, Eastern thought, and everything in between, attempting to adjust my teachings to a different age level can be somewhat intimidating. Sharing these philosophies with adults, however, has always felt more natural to me. I truly love kids, but I know that I'm far more authentic when speaking to middle-aged spiritual seekers.

At the end of my Daisy talk, the girls looked exhausted, and it was obvious that they'd had enough of The Kindness Guy. And to be perfectly honest, I was ready to go home, too. Mentally and physically, I was completely drained. Don't get me wrong; the girls were sweet and their parents were wonderful . . . *but this just wasn't me.* As I leaned against a wall of crayon canvasses, staring at the pile of pink backpacks at my feet, I finally began to realize that this was probably not the ideal audience for my message.

It seemed as if my dreams of becoming a world-renowned speaker were now light-years away, especially since I'd just recalled the details of my "contract" for this presentation. Because the group didn't have money to cover my speaking fee, they'd offered me a unique payment for my services: freshly baked cookies. I can still remember the phone call, agreeing to their proposal, and working on my attitude by thinking, *I'll bet every great inspirational speaker started this way.* Although I'd graciously agreed to *Toll House cookies* as compensation for this talk, my heart was set on a much bigger dream, and a very different house: *Hay House.*

Hay House is the leader when it comes to putting on life-changing events and publishing self-improvement materials. It's also home to some of the world's most acclaimed and inspirational personalities, such as Dr. Wayne W. Dyer, Cheryl Richardson, Deepak Chopra, Dr. Christiane Northrup, and, of course, the amazing founder, Louise Hay. But Hay House is much more than simply a premier company of world-renowned authors and speakers. Their events and products have changed millions of lives and elevated the consciousness of our planet. I can honestly say that their books have not only improved my life, but at one time saved it.

Becoming a part of this family has been my greatest dream. For any author who writes personal-development or metaphysical books, being published by Hay House is the highest honor. For years I've fantasized about sharing a stage with Dr. Wayne Dyer, traveling, speaking to thousands of people, and making a difference in people's lives all over the world.

But let's get real for a moment here. Accomplishing my goal to be a part of the best is something that would obviously take years of hard work, the right connections, and perhaps a lifetime of good karma. Especially for someone like me, who barely graduated from high school, had never taken a writing class in his life, and just two years ago was deathly afraid of public speaking. To think that anyone could make it to the big leagues with such limitations was totally unrealistic. Right?

Well, Not Exactly . . .

I remember the very first time it arrived in my e-mail inbox: *Hay House Presents Movers & Shakers: Building a Multimedia Platform that Brings Your Message to the World! Boston, Massachusetts, April 23–25, 2010.* As you can imagine, I totally flipped out when I found out about this. The thought of having an opportunity to learn from the best and discover new ways to share my message with the world was pure bliss for me. After quickly skimming over the event description, I was convinced that this was exactly what I needed to take my career to the next level. I absolutely *knew* I had to be at this conference, and I needed to buy a ticket *now!* There was simply no way I could take the chance of it selling out. At that point, I ran for the drawer, grabbed my Visa card, logged on to **www.hayhouse.com**, took a big swig of my coffee . . . and soon felt my heart sinking deep into my stomach. "No way," I said out loud. My enthusiasm was quickly tempered by a ticket price of $595 coupled with my less-than-inspiring financial situation.

The reality was that after two and a half years in business, financially speaking, it just wasn't working. Even though The Kindness Center had become a household name; had won awards for school programs; and had received 4,000-plus website hits each month, thousands of Facebook fans, and been getting tons of media coverage, we were still sinking fast. Interest in my work was off the charts, but the money simply wasn't coming in. Each week I was flooded with inquiries and speaking requests, but most of the organizations didn't have the funding to get me through their doors. Since we were still in the midst of a recession, many schools and businesses were cutting their budgets, and professional presentations were the first things to go. I was giving talks each week, but I needed much more lucrative jobs to keep us out of the red.

For months I thought about the Movers & Shakers event. Each week I'd go to their website and think, *This could be the big break I've been waiting for.* It was especially appealing since best-selling author Cheryl Richardson and Hay House president Reid Tracy would be teaching this course. Meeting them and learning their secrets would be the opportunity of a lifetime.

As the weeks flew by and the date of the conference drew near, I'll admit, I was beginning to lose hope. My speaking engagements that were scheduled for the spring were nearly complete, and the chances of new work arriving before April 23 seemed improbable. And despite my wonderful, always-encouraging wife who kept telling me with total conviction, "You are absolutely, positively going to the Movers & Shakers event," I had a difficult time seeing how that could possibly be true. And it was especially unlikely since we were behind on bills and had pretty much melted every credit card we owned. If I was going to make it to Boston in April, it was going to take a complete miracle. . . .

The Month of Miracles

With only four weeks to go before Movers & Shakers, I decided it would be best to relax, and shift from a place of *how* to one of *allow.* I practice this technique when I feel stressed or worried about achieving a certain goal. I've often found that the mantra of *how* can be a major block to my positive energy and ability to manifest what I desire, but whenever I simply put my trust in God/life/the universe and *allow* things to unfold, the right people, circumstances, and, more often than not, amounts of money, always seem to show up.

Allowing, however, does *not* mean sitting around waiting for the magic to appear. There's still work to be done. Between the dozens of e-mails I receive each day, managing The Kindness Center Facebook page, creating newsletters, developing marketing plans, and attending meetings (not to mention trying to change the world), sitting still just isn't an option for me. And this particular day was definitely no exception to this rule.

After wading through my morning e-mails and Facebook messages, I was soon out the door to attend a meeting with a local school. Twice a year, I donate what amounts to a $600 program to a school that simply can't find the funds to pay my speaking fee. It always gives me a lift to be able to help them out, especially since the budget cuts in our educational system have been so immense.

After chatting with the principal and discussing the details of my talk, I left feeling pretty energized. This school really deserved a break, and I was happy to help. But I also have to be truthful about something. During the 30-minute drive back to my office, a somewhat bittersweet thought popped into my head: I realized I'd just given away a $600 speaking fee, which was *the exact amount I needed for the Movers & Shakers conference.* Through my meditation practice, I've learned to watch my mind closely, so I instantly recognized the danger of this type of thinking. I could see that I was about to question the gift I'd just given. As quickly as I could, I gently pushed this thought out of my consciousness, replacing it with a new one: *true kindness is about giving unconditionally and never expecting anything in return.* Yes, sometimes I needed to remember to practice what I preach.

By the next day, I'd pretty much forgotten about the $600 gift and was ready to tackle my daily list of projects. First up for the day was my website. It's a never-ending process, but one that I love. I truly enjoy the creative aspect of web design and seeing my site evolve. Sitting at my desk, I began adding a few lines of text to my home page, when the familiar high-pitched sound of "kerblink" called to me from my e-mail inbox. I'm fairly good at multitasking, so, more often not, I respond to messages quickly so I can keep up with the huge volume I receive daily.

This one happened to be from my dear friend Marie. We had recently been back in touch after she had read an article about me in a local newspaper. She and I go back almost 15 years to a time when we worked at a photo lab together. My career at the lab was pretty short-lived, however, because I wanted to own my own portrait-photography business. But in the year that we worked together, Marie and I had created a very special bond. It was not one having to do with film, camera gear, or the best way to light a portrait; but rather, it was a connection of the spirit, and a passion for discussing the mysteries of the universe.

Shortly after my father died in 2000, Marie did something that would forever change the course of my life. At a time when I was deeply depressed and simply couldn't move past my father's suicide, she gave me a book called *You'll See It When You Believe It.* I remember looking at the cover, noticing the poorly lit author photo, and reading that some guy named Dr. Wayne W. Dyer had written it. After thumbing through a few pages, it became clear to me that this was much more than just another "positive thinking" book. I'd been reading other self-help materials, but for some reason this one felt different. Desperate for anything to pull me out of the black hole I was living in, I decided not only to read it, but to actually do something I hadn't done with other transformational literature I'd read . . . *apply* it.

Marie's simple act of kindness ensured that my life would never be the same again. It also transformed my office into a shrine for just about every book, video, and audio program ever created by Dr. Dyer. He has been the most influential teacher in my life over the past ten years, and his work always seems to find that place deep in my heart that needs healing or a jolt of inspiration.

But as wonderful as Marie's paperback gift was to me back then, I hadn't seen *anything* yet. Even though she'd already been buying the recently self-published version of *am I being kind* for her friends, promoting The Kindness Center, and sending me encouraging notes, her next act of kindness was bigger than anything I could ever have imagined. It also became very clear to me that she wasn't working alone; the entire universe was about to grab me by the collar, look straight into my eyes, and, with unmistakable fervor, say, "Hold on tight, Mike. You're about to go for one hell of a ride!"

Shaking Things Up

Marie is a huge fan of Hay House publications, and especially Louise Hay. So as you can imagine, when I told her about Movers & Shakers, her enthusiasm shot straight through the roof. Not only is this woman a great friend, she's also the queen of creative visualization and positive energy. She would often tell me that she absolutely *knew* (not thought or believed) that my book would be sold in stores. She'd actually gone into many of the booksellers in her area, stared at the shelves, and visualized it sitting among other inspirational titles. On more than one occasion she has said, "It will sell like hotcakes, Mike!"

Through an exchange of e-mails, I told her that I'd most likely be going to the conference in Boston, but I just needed to schedule one more speaking gig in order to purchase a ticket. I didn't want to sound halfhearted, so I did my best to remain in the spirit of Louise Hay's "I can do it" attitude. Marie, however, is incredibly intuitive and has a sensitive soul, and her next e-mail completely blew me away:

> *Hi Mike,*
>
> *Is this the seminar that is this month—April 23–25? Would you still be able to get into it? Let me know, and I'll gladly help you out! This would be a gift, and outsiders do not need to know. I'm not trying to twist your arm . . . but let's chat about this a little more by phone. The Universe works in unexpected ways at times.*
>
> *Love,*
> *Marie*

I was speechless. I just didn't know what to say. My mind screamed, *I can't! This is way too much!* while my heart kept calling out, *Thank you, thank you, thank you!* I felt so torn. I also began thinking about a recent workshop where I'd taught the importance of receiving kindness. "When we reject an act of kindness," I'd said, "the flow of kind energy is blocked and we cheat the individual out of the experience of giving." Damn.

So after a few more e-mails, some arm-twisting, and a two-hour phone conversation, Marie had convinced me that I *needed* to be at this event and that *something magical was going to take place there*. But the magic was already happening, and things just kept getting more interesting.

The day before we spoke, something had sparked Marie's memory, reminding her of an old checking account she hadn't used in years. Deciding that this might be a good time to look at her balance, she was about to get another sign that "the Universe works in unexpected ways." Yes, it was true. The account contained just a hair over the amount that I needed for a ticket.

Two days later, Marie mailed me a check for $600. And on the *very* same day she sent it, she received a letter from an insurance company stating that her cousin, who had passed away two months ago, had made Marie the beneficiary of her life insurance policy. Amazing! Marie saw this as another gift from the universe, called me, and asked if we could meet. Within minutes of getting together, she handed me another check and exclaimed, "This is a gift from Cousin Helen!" Then she tells me that I need to use this money to stay overnight in Boston for the three-day conference rather than drive an hour and 40 minutes each way. "I just know Cousin Helen would be thrilled to give this to you," she says. After a peaceful walk and stopping to admire a sea of daffodils along the way, I drive home with tears streaming down my face, thinking, *What is going on here?*

The embarrassing truth is that just two days prior, my wife was rolling change at the kitchen table while I was bagging our bottle returns to use for tolls and gas money. So to have this kind of abundance flowing into our lives at this moment was a complete miracle. The event ticket, two nights' stay in Boston, food, gas, tolls, and whatever money was left over, Marie said, "was for performing all of those random acts of kindness." It just seemed too good to be true. And as an added bonus, I'd just discovered through a very reliable source that Louise Hay was now planning to attend the entire conference! What an incredible opportunity this would be to meet the woman who had started it all! But believe it or not, the best was yet to come. This was simply the beginning.

• • •   • • •

Chapter 4

Moving & Shaking in Boston

Standing in line at the registration desk was surreal. I couldn't help recalling everything that had happened in order for me to be there. The last four weeks felt like a dream, and I definitely *did not* want to wake up! *But this is real,* I nervously thought. And as proof, I'd just checked into a beautiful hotel only a block from the event center. There was now only one thing I needed to do in order to make this a done deal: *move ten feet forward.* I just needed the pretty blonde woman at the table to give me my registration packet, smile, and say, "You're all set. Have a great weekend!"

But before I could get my hands on that golden ticket, I had to be patient. The lady in front of me seemed confused, was asking questions, and was trying to figure out where to pay. Doing my best to look cool, I began digging through my backpack for a bottle of water. I tried to remain calm, but the truth was that I wanted that damn ticket, *and I wanted it now!* The woman in front of me must have felt my anxiety, for within seconds she stepped aside, turned around, and as she opened her mouth to say, "I'm sorry . . ." we both nearly fell over.

It was Julie. As teenagers, she and I had been long-distance sweethearts. But life, 225 miles, and my being a not-so-kind boyfriend had changed all of that. We hadn't seen each other since my wedding day nearly 12 years before! We'd remained friends through a yearly Christmas card and, more recently, by connecting through Facebook.

That Friday morning, before leaving for the conference, my Facebook status said: "Spending three days immersed in the love and wisdom of the amazing Louise Hay." Julie, who is a spontaneous, spiritual-seeking "nutcase" like me, saw the post, became curious about the event, and within hours found herself in Boston, too. Crazy? Perhaps. It quickly became evident, however, that I wasn't the only one who *needed* to be there. This weekend would prove to be life-changing for Julie as well, but I'll leave that story for her to tell in her own book one day.

Once You Make a Decision

Ralph Waldo Emerson once said: "Once you make a decision, the universe conspires to make it happen." As you'll soon see, this powerful statement is the absolute truth. But because it would take an entire book to relate every moment of this story, I'll be kind to you, dear reader, and offer a somewhat condensed version of this magical ride. Here we go . . .

Friday, April 23, Day 1

I attend the introductory evening program from 7:30 to 9:30 P.M. Within the first 30 minutes, I meet and get a hug from Louise Hay! At 83 years old, she shines brighter than most people who are half her age.

The class then begins with disheartening news: Hay House will accept no manuscripts, book proposals, products, or gifts during this weekend. I mutter the words, "Oh, shit," as I discreetly slide three gift bags and books back into my backpack.

The first class is fantastic, and I'm totally juiced up for the weekend. At 11:00, I head to my hotel feeling totally exhausted and dizzy, with the fiery sensation of a hot coal beginning to settle in the back of my throat. I get the unnerving sensation that something very nasty is on its way. As my head hits the pillow that night, I pray, "Please God, please . . . let me feel better in the morning."

Saturday, April 24, Day 2

I wake up around 5:30 A.M. feeling pretty funky. I'm normally a morning person, but four hours of sleep just doesn't do it for me. I can now feel a major head cold settling in. After a piping-hot shower and some coffee that tastes like jet fuel, I'm determined to make this an extraordinary day. My mantra of "You are totally responsible for your own happiness" rings in my head and, surprisingly, begins to work.

This day is a massive confidence builder for me. All of the information they're giving us about building a platform and making it in this business I've pretty much already done. In two years I've been able to accomplish what most people said would take ten. *Very cool,* I think. At the noon break, my friend Julie and I have lunch together and enjoy a wonderful conversation. I'm trying to remain upbeat, but the truth is I feel like complete hell.

Class starts up again at 1:30, and I'm getting even worse. My head is spinning and my throat is still on fire. I know being here is a huge blessing, so I do everything possible to focus, take good notes, and soak in this once-in-a-lifetime opportunity.

At the end of the day, Cheryl Richardson and Reid Tracy begin teaching a piece on public speaking. They announce that on Sunday morning they'll randomly choose 4 people out of the 130 in attendance to give a seven-minute talk. This exercise is designed to help us learn the proper formula (and gain the necessary confidence) to speak in front of a crowd. And for a chance to be one of the lucky four chosen, all I have to do is simply raise my hand. Hearing that, Julie turns to me and says, "You're doing it!"

I shrug off her comment and mumble, "We'll see," while in my mind I think, *No freakin' way.* Standing up in front of Hay House founder Louise Hay, Reid Tracy, and best-selling author Cheryl Richardson while I'm looking and feeling like this was just *not* going to happen. As they say, you only get one chance at a first impression, and there was no way I was going to blow it here.

The conference ends for the day, and I'm totally wiped out. I feel miserable, but I've really been looking forward to meeting my son this evening for some Mexican food. Alex goes to college in Boston and wants to introduce me to his friends and grab a bite to eat. After we have dinner, I stop at the grocery store to pick up some high-octane cold syrup. Once I drop Alex off at school, I can barely drive myself to the hotel. Through the grace of God (and my brother-in-law's GPS), I somehow make it there around 9:30. Once back in my room, I drink *way* more than the recommended amount that's printed on the label of the liquid medicine and fall asleep to the disheartening thought, *I'm skipping tomorrow's program. I just want to go home.*

Sunday, April 25, Day 3

I've overslept by an hour. It's now just past 6 A.M. I typically like to get up closer to 5 so I can meditate, do yoga, and go for a run. Running is out of the question today, but I actually do feel a new spark of energy. The cold remedy that knocked me out last night also seemed to clear out much of the "yucks." I decide to meditate for ten minutes and then see if some yoga might help even more. It does.

After a shower and some black coffee, my energy is beginning to increase, and I know that I'm going to attend the final day of the conference. But I also feel very *different*. Not in a "you drank too much cold medicine" sort of way, but I have a strange sensation that something *really* good is going to happen today. I can only describe it as a subtle blend of passion and inner peace.

As I leave my hotel room around 8:00, I have an unmistakable new confidence in my step. I'm still not at my best, but it's a far cry from how I felt last night. A few feet from the elevator, something causes me to slow my pace. I can see in my peripheral vision that someone is standing right beside me, and as I turn, the shape is now mimicking my moves and staring back at me like a long-lost friend. "Hey," I say, looking around to make sure we're alone. "You're going to do *great* today. This is *the* opportunity you've been waiting for, and I totally believe in you." Staring deep into his eyes, I smile, and then walk away from the four-foot mirror framed in gold.

At 8:30 I arrive at the event center still with the sensation that this is going to be a special day. Although at this point I haven't convinced myself that I'll be raising my hand this morning, the conversation with the mirror seemed to be an indication that I was perhaps considering it. After saving a chair with my backpack, I decide to make a quick pit stop in the restroom before things get started.

As I'm washing my hands I think, *Hmm, more mirrors, maybe I need to give myself one more pep talk.* But before I can toss myself an extra affirmation, a man I haven't seen all weekend walks through the door, slows down, and stops. Squinting, he looks directly at me, points his finger toward my heart, and declares: "Good luck today." With the slightest hint of a smile and the tone of an old Jedi Master, he repeats: "Good luck today."

Trying to be polite (although I'm completely freaked out), I smile back and respond with a tone of uncertainty as I leave, "Thank you?"

My heart is now racing like a caffeinated greyhound, because I know *exactly* what he meant—*I have to raise my hand.* My mind starts right in: *Your dream is right in front of you! This is the ultimate job interview! You have a chance to present to Louise Hay, Reid Tracy, and Cheryl Richardson!* I know I'll kick myself for the rest of my life if I don't do this, but, honestly, it isn't even about being chosen so much as having the courage to put my hand in the air. Just doing that would be enough. Then, seconds later, a new thought flies in and sucker punches me square in the gut: *If they do choose you, what the hell are you going to talk about!?"* Perhaps I should have asked my bathroom guru a few questions before I rushed out the door. . . .

Around 9:45 Louise Hay kicks off the final day of the conference with a brief talk. She's brilliant.

In addition to discussing the power of self-love and affirmations, her intention is to calm the nerves of those of us in the audience who might be speaking this morning. The story of her very first presentation is so sweet and exactly what we need to hear. Thanks to Louise's soothing voice and peaceful energy, we're all feeling a bit calmer.

The recommended formula for giving a talk (if you're lucky enough to be picked) is simple: the presenter has seven minutes to tell the audience who he or she is, share a compelling story, and then give a call to action for making the world a better place. Only four people will be chosen. It's totally random, and neither Cheryl nor Reid know anything about us, or what our abilities are.

After anxiously watching three solid performances, my math skills kick in as I realize, *Three down, one to go*. I absolutely *know* what's coming next. I quickly lean toward Julie, who is sitting next to me, and whisper, "Here, take this."

Her expression says, "Huh, what do you need?" Looking down, she sees that I'm holding my iPod Touch with a small microphone plugged into it. Keeping my voice low, I quickly explain how to work the device, saying, "Just hit this, open that, and then tap this RECORD button." There's *no way* I'm going to miss archiving what's about to take place.

The moment Cheryl hands Reid the microphone to choose the last speaker, I know it's me . . . not because he looks my way or even gives the slightest hint that I'm on deck, but because I've finally figured out what the last month has been all about. This is such a huge "Aha!" moment for me. I now understand that everything that has taken place over the past four weeks was not luck, coincidence, or even karma. It's so much bigger than that. I finally realized the mind-blowing truth: *My dreams wanted me just as much as I wanted them! Yes, I am my dream's dream!* I am what they long for with each beat of their heart. They have been calling out to me every single day, and all of the so-called coincidences during this time have actually been moments of grace and the universe saying, "I'm here. I'm ready for you!" Knowing this, there were only three things left to do: take a deep breath, open my hand . . . and simply say, "Yes."

Within seconds, Reid and the microphone are directly in front of me. *Yes,* my inner voice roars, *Yes!* Jumping to my feet, I feel nothing but pure, energetic bliss. There are no nerves, no head cold, not even the slightest concern that I'm about to give *the* most important performance of my life. And although I own a huge repertoire of stories from my 40-year roller-coaster ride, I know that there's only one I want to share today: the one that started it all, the turtle story.

Without hesitation, I shoot to the front of the room and rock the house. I deliver a talk that would soon become one of the most significant moments of my professional career. Looking into the crowd, I see wonder in everyone's eyes—even Louise, Reid, and Cheryl. Throughout my time onstage, I continue looking their way, simply letting them know that I'm totally confident and that I was born to be a speaker.

After seven minutes of heaven, a thunderous ovation blows the roof off the event center. Louise Hay, just ten feet from me, places her hands next to her heart, smiles softly, and looks at me as if to say, "I'm so proud of you" (words I eventually hear from her later that day). It's amazing, absolutely *amazing*. Trying to remain calm, I continue to soak it all in while the words *You did it; you really did it!* dance in my head. Looking into the crowd, I can now see Julie's face beaming back at me. Her sparkling eyes say two things: "I am *so* proud of you, Mike!" and "Yes, I *did* press Record!"

Monday, April 26

Cheryl Richardson sends me an e-mail asking me to be a special guest on Hay House Radio.

Tuesday, April 27

Reid Tracy e-mails me, requesting a copy of my self-published book to review and asking if Hay House could possibly fit into my future plans. (Seriously!?)

Monday, May 3

Reid e-mails again and wants to know if we can have a phone conversation on Thursday. Ten thousand butterflies find a new home in my stomach.

Tuesday, May 4

I wake up to Facebook messages and e-mails from friends screaming at me: "Wayne Dyer is 'tweeting' about you and your book on Twitter!"

I click on the link to his page and instantly blurt out the words "Holy shit!" I later find out that Reid had a little something to do with this incredible act of kindness.

Thursday, May 6

I have a great conversation with Reid. After about ten minutes (and still not 100 percent sure what's happening), I boldly ask the big question: "So can I tell my mom this weekend (Mother's Day) that I'm going to be a Hay House author and speaker?"

Reid chuckles and says, "Yes."

Monday, May 10

I receive a publishing contract from Hay House . . . *on Wayne Dyer's 70th birthday.*

From My Journey . . . to Your Journey

Although it wasn't always my way of thinking, I now see how each experience in my life simply had to happen for my story to unfold as it has so far. It's clear to me that *every* moment has significance and is part of the universal perfection. Yes, I'm grateful for *all* of it—the good, the bad, and even the extremely ugly. I can now see that everything has been a tremendous gift.

My new attitude, however, tends to make people curious, whether it's those who have known me for 25 years or are just hearing my story for the first time. One of the most frequent questions I am asked is: "How did you go from depression, suicidal tendencies, and sleeping in a car to living out your dreams?" The answer to that is the very purpose of this book.

In Parts II and III that follow, it's my intention to reveal exactly how I shifted from a place of misery to now living an inspired new life. Although it may sound too simplistic, you'll soon discover that consistent happiness is a result of the decisions you make. In Part II, I want to offer you the same critical choices that have helped me overcome past challenges, create authentic joy, and achieve the dream you just read about. Making these changes will also lead you to a vastly kinder life. Part III then shows you how a truly benevolent lifestyle will play out . . . *and its extraordinary benefits.*

I believe passionately in these principles because I know they work for almost anyone, no matter what path he or she might be on. I also know that if you follow the steps outlined in each chapter, it will help ignite your own spirit and allow you to manifest your heart's every desire.

• • •   • • •

part ii

Seven Choices That Will Change Your Heart, Your Life . . . and Your World

Chapter 5

The First Choice: Being Responsible or Being a Victim

"It's the economy, my parents, my boss, my ex, the government, God, genetics, my bad knees . . . *it's just not my fault!*" It's safe to say that we all know someone who sounds like this. This kind of thinking is perhaps our biggest contributor not only to personal challenges, but to global issues as well. By blaming everyone else and not taking responsibility for what happens to us, we take on the classic role of the victim. Unfortunately, to act in this way is to give up all control in our lives.

Victims love to complain, gossip, and spread rumors; they thrive on tension, and they can't stop talking about what's wrong with the world. Their "hobbies" include family feuds, friction with co-workers, self-pity, and constantly seeking approval. Turmoil is like a narcotic to these people—the more negativity there is in their lives, the better! But drama simply reinforces a neurotic belief that they possess, which is that *they* are never the problem; everyone else is.

In addition to relentlessly blaming the entire universe for what has happened to them (or in many cases, blaming it on plain old "bad luck"), those who take on the role of scapegoat also weaken their connection to their spiritual source. It makes no difference whether that source is called God, the Big Guy, the Great Mother, or Higher Intelligence, its energy is our direct link to the truth of who we are: *powerful creators*. When we play the victim card, we're not trusting in ourselves or the wisdom that created us. This outlook causes fear to become our constant companion.

Personal responsibility is the opposite of playing the victim. To be responsible means that you are in complete control and accept the role of creator of your life. My meditation teacher once offered me an insight that complements this point nicely: "Some people pursue happiness, while others create it." Creators understand this and know that it's not what happens to them in life, but how they respond that's important. Therefore, external circumstances and major challenges can only become painful and frustrating through an unnatural perspective or the conditioned belief: "It's not my responsibility, and it's not my fault!" The analytical mind loves this idea, but your true nature knows that you and you alone determine your level of happiness.

The Optimist and the Pessimist

There's a wonderful little story about seven-year-old twin boys. One was a complete pessimist, the other a total optimist. Worried about their extreme personalities, their mother decided to take them to a psychiatrist.

First, the doctor attempted to treat the pessimistic boy who was always crying, complaining, and miserable no matter what the circumstances were. In an effort to brighten his outlook on life, the psychiatrist took him to a room that was piled to the ceiling with brand-new toys. "They're all for you!" he exclaimed with zeal. For the next couple of minutes, the child looked carefully at the toys, but instead of tearing open the boxes and playing with delight, he burst into tears.

"What's the matter?" the psychiatrist asked, baffled by this meltdown. "Don't you want to play with any of your new toys?"

"Yes!" the little boy screamed, "but this one says it's for ages nine and up, and I'm only seven. And this one says it needs batteries, and I didn't bring any! And this one says I need to assemble it, and I don't know how!" Quite concerned by the child's attitude, the doctor informed the mother that treatment would likely be necessary.

Next, the psychiatrist began to work with the other twin, the eternal optimist. He was the complete opposite of his brother, and nothing seemed to bring him down. Trying to dampen his outlook, this boy was taken to a room that was full of fresh horse manure. Certain that this would upset him, the doctor said, "It's all for you, son. This is my gift to you!"

But rather than looking at the pile of dung with disgust, the child's eyes sparkled with excitement. Seconds later, he jumped eagerly into the foul-smelling mound and began joyfully digging out scoop after scoop with his bare hands. Totally confused and quite concerned about the boy's well-being, the psychiatrist screamed, "What do you think you're doing?!"

Wiping himself off, the little optimist looked up with enthusiasm and exclaimed, "With all this manure, there *must* be a pony in here somewhere!"

The Real Meaning

Many people have heard a version of this story, but they don't often take it to the next level. If they did, they'd realize that it's all about the power of perspective. Choosing to view the world with optimism, and having the ability to "find the pony" within the challenges that come our way, is truly what this chapter is all about. Sadly, many of us decide to remain mired in the "pile" and waste our time complaining about it. This is the victim's point of view, and it's one that can never lead to a more joyous and kinder life.

Then there are those who simply can't stand the smell of manure for more than a day or two before deciding that there's another way to view their problems. These are the people who see the bigger picture, grab a shovel, and start digging! They understand that moving through issues is what ultimately leads to *self-discovery* (they grow personally and spiritually through their challenges), *compassion* (their heart now goes out to those in similar situations), and *wisdom* (they gain the experience and insight to help others).

The Power to Choose

Perhaps the greatest gift we've been given as creative beings is the power of choice. We make thousands of choices every single day—whether they're regarding the people we associate with, our careers, the words we speak, the clothes we wear, or which street we choose to walk down. Each of our lives is an accumulation of the decisions we've made. The power of choice is what makes us ordinary or extraordinary, and to be a conscious chooser is to have the ability to manifest or alter anything we wish.

Deciding to take total responsibility was my first step toward a life that was no longer riddled with blame and conflict. Whether it was my depression or my financial demise, I was no longer willing to point my finger at the rest of the world. After choosing to be 100 percent accountable for *everything* that came my way, my circumstances began to change.

I now know that it's up to me to manage my emotions, career, finances, relationships, and even my ability to lose a few pounds. This outlook gave me an overwhelming sense of confidence, which translated into many new friends and great opportunities.

I learned that responsibility is an attractive quality, especially since people were asking me for advice.

I also discovered that it meant occasionally needing to swallow my pride and say five very challenging words from time to time: "I'm sorry" and "I was wrong."

This is one of the most difficult yet liberating things you can do in your interactions with others. Admitting that you were wrong is an absolute must if you'd like to live peacefully, and this is true whether you're dealing with an issue in your marriage or sitting in rush-hour traffic. Letting go of your need to be right ends conflict instantly and drowns the ego's desire to be "better than."

Is this easy? Absolutely not. But with time and honest self-observation, it will not only become possible, it will also seem natural. After all, this is how you first arrived in the world. When you were born, you were never interested in being right or superior to others. The true, unconditioned self wants cooperation rather than competition.

The Heart's Perspective

At times people will argue against this first choice, *being responsible or being a victim,* by asking, "How can you say I'm not a victim if I was hit by a runaway bus?" "What about getting cancer from the factory that's been pumping chemicals into the air?" or "How about when my doctor made the wrong call during surgery?" This, of course, is the mind desperately needing to be right and making someone else wrong. When you choose not to take this point of view, it doesn't mean that you are disregarding what is happening to you; rather, you're changing your perspective, recognizing how the challenge creates growth, and seeing how it can help others. With this attitude, a so-called curse is now seen as a blessing.

While I do feel that being responsible for our own thoughts is essential to kinder living, there are certain cases when a person can't make positive choices so easily. I was recently taught this lesson while at my mom's house on Mother's Day.

While standing in my mother's kitchen helping her fix lunch, I could see that my stepfather, whom I'll call Kevin, had just arrived with a guest. Looking out the window onto the front yard, I saw a man, perhaps in his 50s, awkwardly following Kevin around to the side of the house. I'd never seen this guy before, so I just assumed that he was a neighbor or a friend. Not thinking too much about it, I continued with the meal preparations.

Moments later, the door flew open and the visitor who'd been following Kevin was now in the lead.

Rushing through the kitchen, this tall, lanky stranger moved his body with such urgency that it became clear he was on a *very* important mission. What exactly that mission was, I honestly hadn't the faintest idea. But as his laser-sharp eyes cut through the room, I knew he wanted something, and he wanted it badly.

Lifting his pointy chin, he looked to the side and let out his first words. "I like cooooffffeeeee," he squawked. His voice, which had a birdlike quality to it, sounded like a raspy old crow or a pterodactyl from the Jurassic period. "I like cooooffffeeeeee," he repeated. I now understood that his mission was to acquire the nearest ceramic mug and fill it with the black caffeine brewing directly to his right.

It turned out that his name was Jesse, and he'd been under Kevin's care for the past six years. Kevin, who exudes kindness, works with mentally and physically challenged individuals who need assistance with everyday living. In addition to making them coffee, cooking them meals, and assisting with the not-so-pleasant task of personal hygiene, he offers so much more. His gifts of compassion and patience are probably his greatest qualifications for this job. Besides helping Jesse with his daily routines, Kevin also takes him on walks and occasional day trips—basically doing whatever is necessary for him to experience the highest quality of life.

After finally receiving his cup of joe, Jesse sat at the kitchen table for the next 30 minutes, taking sips while spinning the blue and gray mug in his crooked hands. Still not knowing anything about him, I watched him flip thumb over thumb while still turning the mug at a dizzying pace. I later discovered that this was simply his unique way of calming his nerves . . . but it sure wasn't helping mine.

I was both curious and a little nervous about this stranger who was now sitting 15 feet away from me. I wanted to say "Hello," but I still couldn't decide if eye contact was a good idea. I'd spent time around people with mental disabilities before, and I'd found that each person has his or her own set of "rules." For example, I knew a man with Down syndrome who would hug me like there was no tomorrow. But I've also met individuals who would scream upon receiving the lightest tap on their shoulder. Knowing this, I felt that it was best to keep my distance and ask my mother about him once he and Kevin left.

After spending some time with my brother-in-law in the next room, Kevin finally walked back into the kitchen. Realizing that we'd never met before, he initiated an introduction. "Jesse, have you met Mike?"

Okay, I thought, *this would surely tell me something.*

"I like cooofffeeeee!" he cried out. My mom leaned over to tell me that his vocabulary pretty much consisted of that one word along with an occasional "ice cream." Kevin spoke up again. "Jesse, come meet Mike."

Jesse sprang up from his chair as if on a pogo stick, and my heart started racing. Now walking straight toward me, he displayed the same intensity in his steps I'd seen during his initial entry just an hour before. His body language and powerful momentum also had me bracing myself just in case he didn't stop in time . . . but he did. With just inches between his face and mine, Jesse abruptly came in close and did the very last thing I expected him to do: *he looked straight into my eyes.* And this was more than just your typical eye contact. It was one of those rare eye locks where neither person felt uncomfortable nor had any desire to look down or away. His gaze was hypnotic. Seconds later, his right hand rose from his side and was offered to me. Raising mine to accept his invitation, I simply said, "Very nice to meet you."

Holding my hand while still looking deep into my eyes, he took in a breath, exhaled, and responded with his life's mantra: "I like cooofffeeeee."

After our brief introduction, Jesse quickly found his way back to the table. As I turned to my mom, she was now smiling, looking at me with an expression that said, "See, he's harmless."

I'll admit it, I did feel a little better. Now understanding his rules and boundaries, I was much more relaxed. But I also felt somewhat guilty and, especially, judgmental. I wished I hadn't allowed myself to feel fear and uncertainty in the first place. Turning back toward the table, I could see that Jesse was still looking my way. His lips, curled slightly upward, gave the subtle hint of a smile, while his eyes remained connected to mine. Still keeping one hand on his lukewarm coffee cup, he gently lifted his other hand, waving to me as if he were sitting atop a float in a parade. "I like coooffffeeeee."

A few minutes later, my mom, still putting the finishing touches on our lunch, conspiratorially leaned toward me. "Do you know what happened to him?" Her words instantly shocked me and created a feeling of unease. Careful not to bring attention to our conversation, she whispered again, "You know, he wasn't always this way."

"What do you mean?" I nervously asked.

"I mean he wasn't born this way." Still speaking softly, Mom began to tell me that Jesse had been a perfectly healthy little boy until the age of ten. Looking across the room, she now gestured toward my ten-year-old nephew and quietly continued. "He was once just like Andrew—happy, healthy, and playful." At this point, I wasn't sure I really wanted to know what had happened. I'd just assumed Jesse was born this way, and I couldn't imagine that his condition was the result of some kind of accident. I got the impression that this story had heartbreak written all over it . . . and it did.

When Jesse was just a child, his father, in a moment of insanity and fury, forever changed the course of his son's life. While the reason is still unclear, this man had pinned the boy to the ground, wrapped both hands around his neck, depleted his last breath, and . . . left him for dead. Now at the age of 58, Jesse's last image as a healthy-minded, normally functioning human being was the sight of his father's enraged face as he attempted to choke the life out of his ten-year-old body. That was Jesse's last day of thinking, speaking, or walking without difficulty. The result of this horrific act was an innocent little boy being forced to live with permanent brain damage for the rest of his life.

My heart shattered into a million pieces. I was also ashamed of my initial, cautious attitude toward him. Fortunately, this feeling didn't last very long, as compassion was now the dominating force in my heart. The immensity of Jesse's situation completely destroyed my model of a "mentally challenged person." I now only saw the divine within this man and recognized him as a spiritual being—especially when I looked into his eyes. By seeing beyond his external conditions and looking into "the windows of his soul," my heart, which just seconds before had been breaking, was now wide open. All fear was now replaced by the power of unconditional love.

• • •

This encounter was also an obvious sign that God had shown up in a clever disguise to reveal an area of my life that still needed work. Ninety-five percent of the time I'm open and very accepting toward everyone I meet, but it was now clear that Jesse had been sent to me to reveal the other five percent. I truly believe that every single person, animal, and living thing on Earth is God attempting to teach us a spiritual lesson. For example, if an aggressive driver upsets us in traffic, that's God teaching us patience. When the teenager with green hair and 15 piercings offends us, that's God offering us a lesson in being nonjudgmental. Or when a 58-year-old disabled man who screams "I like coooofffeeeee" every five minutes makes us feel uneasy and distant . . . that's God teaching us acceptance, compassion, and love.

Soon after learning the truth about Jesse, I found myself sitting with him, attempting to have a conversation about his love for coffee while frequently refilling his mug. At one point, I removed the blue *am I being kind* wristband that I've worn for years and offered it to him as a gift. After Jesse accepted it (and unsuccessfully tried to stretch it over his head), Kevin helped him place it on his left wrist. I suddenly felt so close to this man, and it was difficult to believe that just an hour before I'd exhibited such uncertainty toward him. I only wish I could have looked at him with love right from the beginning. Not only would I have avoided my own personal suffering, but I also would have had an extra hour with a wonderful new friend. Thankfully, the lesson I was able to take away from this event was the ability to recognize the profound difference between the intellectual mind and the heart's perspective.

There are times when someone has been victimized and can't move through his or her predicament very easily. Obviously, the attitude of *"I am 100 percent responsible for my own happiness"* isn't always possible if we aren't blessed with a healthy mind, as in Jesse's case. But is his mind *really* not "healthy"? Consider this: despite the fact that he's limited in most areas of his life; will never marry or have children; and can't work, communicate, drive a car, or even live on his own, *he didn't complain once.* Here's a person who has every reason to be filled with anger and resentment, yet he finds bliss each day in a single cup of coffee. It really makes one wonder. Perhaps one man's "disability" is another man's enlightenment.

Which Picture Do You See?

Once in a while, I'll make the mistake of getting caught up in watching the national news—which is, in my opinion, not always a good way to begin the day. Although I find ways to stay informed about world events, rarely do I tune in to the glorified dismay broadcast by the media. In order to maintain a positive outlook and continue to deliver my lectures with enthusiasm, I find it best to stick to the weather and how the Red Sox did the night before (although if they lose to the Yankees, that can actually dampen my mood for a day).

On one particular occasion, though, I found myself trapped by a story. (If you're a pet owner, you'll surely understand why I couldn't change the channel.) It was about a six-week-old puppy that had been intentionally thrown from a moving car onto a busy highway. He had been badly injured and instantly became a target for other drivers who may not have had time to react to what had just happened. It seemed as if this poor little guy had no chance of surviving. Soon after witnessing the vicious act, though, passersby began to stop; and one woman got out of her car, heroically rescued the puppy, and called for help. Her compassionate heart, along with the kindness of a veterinarian who donated the majority of a $3,000 surgery, ensured that this little dog would not only live, but would run and play again very soon.

While this unfortunate event had a happy ending, it also had a profound threefold effect on me during the 120 seconds it was on the air. First, there was heartbreak from seeing the puppy suffer, next came joy for his survival; and finally, absolute rage toward the person who committed the horrendous crime. I just couldn't understand how someone could be so cruel. I was furious. As a dog lover, the story haunted me all day. Furthermore, I couldn't find a way to let go of the fact that the scoundrel who did this got away.

What followed was even worse—I had the sensation of absolute hopelessness. After seeing such a horrible act of unkindness, I felt beaten down and actually began to question my life's mission of creating a kinder world. Wondering if I was really making a difference, I thought, *Is it really worth it? How can I possibly make an impact with people like that out there?* I was ashamed of my thoughts, discouraged, and somewhat depressed.

Later that afternoon, still needing to vent about the coldhearted puppy assailant, something compelled me to tell my teenage son what had occurred. In medialike fashion, I recounted the story, perhaps hoping to bring him down with me. (Misery does love company, after all.) But as I angrily reported the news to him, expecting agreement with my "What's the world coming to" attitude, I received the lesson of a lifetime.

Without any hesitation, Alex said, "Dad, you keep focusing on that one guy and the unkind thing he did. What about the people who stopped to help, the woman who rescued the dog, and the vet who saved his leg? Don't you see that there was more kindness happening on that day than unkindness?"

I was dumbfounded. He'd taken a day's worth of mental suffering and transformed it in a matter of seconds. By simply changing my perspective, his words ultimately changed my heart. Thanks to the amazing wisdom of my son, this fresh viewpoint sent my spirit soaring and gave me a renewed sense of hope—yes, the world is full of good people; and yes, this mission is worth it.

Shifting Your Perspective

The well-known author Erica Jong once wrote: "Take your life in your own hands, and what happens? A terrible thing: no one to blame." The following examples are situations that show two different perspectives. One is the victim's view, while the other is the heart's perspective of personal responsibility.

A young woman is continually abused (verbally) by her spouse.

Victim: She accepts her situation, and at times even believes his unkind words are true.

Responsibility: She chooses to leave him, take control of her life, and work at a shelter for abused women.

A man is unjustly fired from his job.

Victim: He becomes angry with everyone around him and remains bitter for years.

Responsibility: He chooses to see this event as an opportunity to do something he actually loves.

An 80-year-old woman is mugged in her neighborhood.
Victim: She vows to never go outside again due to her fear of strangers.

Responsibility: She chooses to start a neighborhood watch program and take a class in self-defense.

A mother loses her daughter in a car accident that was caused by a drunk driver.
Victim: She chooses to remain depressed for years, while harboring hatred toward the drunk driver.

Responsibility: She creates a support group for other parents who have lost children to drunk drivers.

A man experiences the heartbreak of a painful divorce.
Victim: He refuses to ever trust women again and vows to never remarry.

Responsibility: He chooses to move forward; and knows that with time, healing, and forgiveness, he will one day learn to love again.

As you can see, there's tremendous power when you shift your perspective from a place of suffering to one of service. If you feel that you've ever been a victim in your life, it's time to change that belief right now. Moving from an egocentric "poor me" role to a place of contribution transforms weakness into strength. When you look at all of your past hurts, big or small, as an opportunity to serve others, you'll become a powerful creator and accept full responsibility for your circumstances.

Making the Choice

You've read about two different ways to experience life. One is to see yourself as a victim, while the other is to take personal responsibility and be in control. Read the following descriptions carefully, and then choose the way you'd like to live.

When I play the victim, my mind makes me think I'm: being betrayed, hurt, burned, scammed, robbed, helpless, wounded, weak, cheated, disliked, or powerless; suffering; or lacking support.

I find myself: acting bitter and irresponsible; being a chronic complainer who's avoided by others; or feeling angry, afraid, or depressed.

When I choose to take personal responsibility, I know I'll be: loved, powerful, creative, in control, admired, respected, healthy, caring, positive, making a difference in the world, supported by others, enjoying many fulfilling relationships, inspired, kind, and loving my life!

Questions for the Heart

Begin by recalling an experience that left you feeling victimized or hurt in some way. Next, turn this feeling around by reflecting on the following questions. Then write down any thoughts or responses you have in your notebook or journal.

- What evidence of growth, compassion, and wisdom can I find in this challenge?

- How could this perspective be helpful to me?

- Am I being kind to myself and others by embracing this new perspective?

• • •

If you agree that an attitude of personal responsibility is the kinder choice, complete the contract with yourself and sign your name.

I have chosen to take personal responsibility for my life because I want to experience more _____

_____

_____.

Your signature _____

Date _____

Choice now made: *Responsibility*

Now that you've taken the path of responsibility—the first crucial choice in building a life of kindness—it's time to move on to exploring forgiveness and its shadow: resentment.

• • •   • • •

Chapter 6

The Second Choice: Forgiveness or Resentment

Marie frantically called her husband . . . but there was no answer. She tried again, but he still didn't pick up. Finally returning her call from his cell phone, Charles told his wife that he wouldn't be coming home that night. Steeped in hatred, he told her about the suicide notes he'd left behind, while also revealing a dark secret from his past. Marie had no idea what he was talking about, but there was obviously something haunting him. Moments later, Charles Carl Roberts IV opened fire on a one-room Amish schoolhouse in Paradise Township, Pennsylvania, and shot 11 young girls, killing 5. In the end, the lone gunman, a 32-year-old milk-truck driver, took his own life just before police moved in.

On October 2, 2006, this tragic story circulated around the world, leaving people heartbroken and in complete shock. The questions *How?* and *Why?* remained central for days, until the grace of the victims' close relatives created an even greater shock.

The grieving families of the five young girls, along with their entire Amish community, did something that seemed totally incomprehensible: they forgave the killer. Not only did they forgive the cruelty of the gunman's acts on that day, but they also reached out in kindness to his family.

Despite feeling the anguish of losing their own children, the Amish people quickly realized that Roberts's wife and children were also casualties of the shooting—they'd lost a husband, a father, and their privacy. At his funeral, more than half of the 75 mourners were Amish. And when a fund was set up to help his family, many from the Amish settlement donated to it. The world was deeply touched by this unbelievable act of kindness, as the headline of "Amish Massacre" was now replaced with "Amish Grace and Forgiveness."

Living in the Now

Most people will categorically agree that one of the most difficult emotions to express is forgiveness. More lives have been destroyed by bitterness and the inability to forgive than perhaps any other negative emotion. Even the most minuscule issues that we refuse to let go of can poison us for a lifetime.

When it comes to this issue, I've found an ancient quote from the Buddha very helpful: "Holding on to anger is like grasping a hot coal with the intent of throwing it at someone else—you are the one who gets burned."

Resentment from my own past was like dragging around a thousand-pound anchor in the form of hostility and self-pity—it became exhausting. Each day I became more and more depleted, as I simply refused to let go of any hurtful actions that had been allegedly perpetrated upon me. Occasionally, I'd find a place in my heart where I wanted to let go, but the tremendous weight on my shoulders wouldn't let me even entertain the thought of it.

As strong as my bitterness toward those around me was, the anger I directed at myself was much worse. Self-hatred consumed me like a cancer, eating away at my soul with every memory of regret. Each time I revisited the past and recalled my mistakes, the burden of carrying this load made my heart grow weaker and weaker.

Self-resentment truly is the original "heart disease"; and to achieve a life of kindness, holding on to this paralyzing energy is simply not an option.

Forgiveness is the key that releases us from the ego's cage and sets us free from the illusions of our past. To forgive, we must first learn to be present, and this means letting go of the past and not anticipating the future—or as Ram Dass told us in the '70s: "Be here now."

The delusional belief in anything other than the present moment is what causes us to feel emotional pain and fear what may or may not happen. The truth is, the only way you can ever experience either one is in your mind. The past is simply a movie you keep replaying in your head, while the future is nothing more than a coming attraction for a film that's yet to be released. Being in the present, however, is the very essence of life and where everything takes place. To completely understand this principle means to recognize that it's impossible to continue to be hurt by anything that has ever happened to you.

The Heart's Perspective

One of the most effective ways in which you can forgive adversaries is by looking at them with sincere compassion. Until you change your perspective and realize that those who have hurt you are also in pain, you'll never be free of resentment.

When working with schools, I always encourage staff and students to embrace this philosophy when dealing with bullies. I honestly believe that someone only becomes a bully because he or she has been abused in some way. Aggression is typically stored-up pain that's released upon an innocent bystander. In most cases, this conduct is an oppressor's cry for help. Rather than attempting to relieve this angst, our culture tends to first punish the offending students. Sadly, this only adds to their negative energy, causing them to repeat their behavior and prolonging the suffering.

My message to our educational system is to stop being *against* bullies and instead be *for* kindness in our schools. Being "for" gives us tremendous strength, while, in my experience, being "against" only weakens us.

For example, even though I watched alcohol destroy my family, I'm not against substance abuse;

I'm *for* healthy living. While I've had friends experience the horrors of war, I'm not against it; I'm *for* peace. And despite having personally witnessed violent acts of unkindness, I'm not against violence; I'm *for* love, compassion, and kindness.

Forgiving my father became a genuine possibility when I was no longer *against* him; and I was only able to do so when I began looking at him with empathy. For me, viewing life through his eyes was now freeing and illuminating . . . but it was also quite heartbreaking. As I began to see the pain inflicted on him by my grandfather, I couldn't help but sympathize and feel an overwhelming sense of compassion toward him. Rather than being angry with my father, I was now opening my heart to him through my awareness of how difficult his life must have been. I didn't think of him as a bully anymore; I knew that he was the one who had been bullied.

This all happened because I was able to change my perspective. By shifting from my head to my heart, everything looked completely different, and my life felt lighter.

We can practice this technique with anyone who has mistreated us. By looking at people in this way, we can see that they're spiritual beings disguised as a mother, a father, a friend, a co-worker, or even a stranger; and they're doing the very best they can. It's not wise to judge others' actions until we truly know their story.

If others have been unkind to you, consider that they may have been hurt in some way. Their harmful actions could simply be a manifestation of the pain in their own hearts and minds. By seeing them as wounded beings, the targets of unkindness themselves, your heart will open . . . which allows a forgiving spirit to flow through you.

Shifting Your Perspective

Perhaps the greatest delusion people experience by refusing to forgive is that they believe it only hurts their enemy. The truth is that if someone has hurt you, hating this person not only punishes him or her, but also lodges this poisonous emotion deeper into your own heart. Over time, this will destroy you, while the accused eventually moves forward in life. Furthermore, showing compassion and forgiving *does not* condone unkind actions in any way. Letting go of the negative behavior never means that you're saying, "Oh, it's fine that you beat, cheated, or hurt me."

Let me be extremely clear: *Justifying the offense is not what forgiveness is about.* Forgiveness is simply a spiritual tool for releasing toxic feelings that keep you from reaching your full human potential. Those who understand this universal truth live happy and healthy lives filled with positive relationships and the gift of inner peace. And this all becomes possible through compassion.

Consider exploring a new perspective with respect to those who have hurt you. See them as . . .

- . . . young children who were perhaps treated in an unkind manner or possibly abused at one time.

- . . . lonely and sad.

- . . . unhappy in their relationships, careers, and lives.

- . . . lacking meaningful friendships.

- . . . filled with regret.

- . . . insecure and having low self-esteem because they've been hurt, too.

- . . . being very sorry for hurting you, but afraid to talk about it.

- . . . being in tremendous pain and simply wanting to be loved.

- ... embarrassed and angry with themselves.

- ... depressed.

- ... missing you and wanting another chance.

In his book *You Can Be Happy No Matter What*, best-selling author Richard Carlson, Ph.D., challenges his readers to ask themselves the simple question: "Do I want to be 'right' or 'happy'?" Dr. Wayne Dyer has also said: "When you have a choice to be right or to be kind, pick kind, and push the ego's demand out of the way." By shifting from the ego's need to be right to a more sympathetic and compassionate heart, you'll set yourself and those you're resenting free. Starting today, begin to look at your past injuries as opportunities to show empathy toward those who have hurt you.

Making the Choice

The following portraits describe two different people. One is resentful and can't let go of the past, while the other chooses to forgive. Their experiences differ with respect to their approaches to life. Read each description carefully, then decide which path you'd like to take.

As a person who continues to be resentful, I see myself as: a victim, weak, hurt, wounded, suffering, paralyzed, or powerless.

I often feel: stressed, angry, anxious, furious, or vengeful.

And I'm afraid others see me as: hostile, bitter, negative, mean, untrusting, a complainer, irritable, or a heart attack waiting to happen.

As a person who chooses to be forgiving, I feel: peaceful, happy, loving, caring, compassionate, empathetic, open-minded, openhearted, strong, in control, and admired.

I know I can be: an inspirational figure, a role model, healthy, positive, emotionally balanced, and kind.

And I have: a strong connection to my friends and family.

Questions for the Heart

Recall a situation where you've been unable to completely forgive. This can involve another person or even yourself. How does being resentful make you feel? Next, turn this feeling around by answering the following questions. Then write down any thoughts or responses you have in your notebook or journal.

- Am I willing to at least consider forgiving myself/this person?

- What could be my new, compassionate perspective of the person who has hurt me?

- Am I being kind to myself and others by embracing this new perspective?

• • •

If you agree that forgiveness is the kinder choice, complete the contract with yourself and sign your name.

I have chosen to begin forgiving myself and others now because I want to experience more _____

_____

_____ *in my life.*

Your signature _____

Date _____

Choices now made: *responsibility* and *forgiveness*

You've now developed the necessary skills that will free you from negative energy and the lingering effects of past resentments. In the following chapter, you'll investigate the next choice in your journey— wellness or abuse.

Chapter 7

The Third Choice: Wellness or Abuse

I'd been gasping for air for over an hour, and things just weren't getting any better—I knew I was in *big* trouble. Years of not taking care of myself had finally caught up with me. My chest felt as if an elephant had parked an SUV on top of it, as the asthma attack to end all asthma attacks was descending upon me. Serious episodes of not being able to breathe had tormented me throughout my life, but this one felt different. With each attempt to fill my lungs with air, the room became darker and the muscles in my back felt as if they'd surely explode. Wheezing, breathless, and filled with terror, I made one final effort to breathe. Seconds later, the whole world went black as I saw the inevitable closing in on me—I was going to die. And I did. . . .

The gravel path was really nothing very special. It was narrow, quite worn, and not exactly what I'd envisioned for my walk toward eternity. I can't really say that I was disappointed; but with all of the talk of a tunnel, bright lights, and music, I guess I was expecting something a bit more "heavenly." The radiant yellow field to my right, however, was another story. Sprinkled with a flower species that I couldn't identify, this buttery meadow also glowed with tall, swaying grass; a few distant trees; and dozens of familiar faces.

Gathered in this sea of gold were all of the people who were dear to me. I'd always expected the afterlife to be filled with those whom I'd lost, but this assembly was complete with family members and friends who were (when I left, anyway) still alive. Each individual looked quite serene and, surprisingly, showed no sign of joy or sadness.

The path, which now seemed more like a conveyor belt, carried me over a small rustic bridge without a single friend or family member attempting to communicate with me. Suddenly, I could also see that this trail of destiny was about to end. It had finally merged with the yellow field; and I now saw a massive, medieval-looking wooden door right in front of me.

As I stood there, I noticed something happening to me that hadn't taken place throughout this entire journey—I was now *feeling*. From the time of my initial blackout up until arriving at the door, I hadn't even felt the slightest hint of emotion. Standing here, however, this was not the case. I saw no one, heard no voices, and received no instructions—I simply knew I had to make a decision. I can remember a sense of panic wash over me as I realized what this was all about: opening the door meant there was no turning back.

• • •

Eighteen hours after it all began, I opened my eyes to find myself strapped to a hospital bed with a hose protruding from a gaping hole in my chest. Connected to the hose, and placed slightly to my right, was a machine pumping air into my lungs—a machine I thought I'd seen once before on an episode of *ER*.

Utter confusion surged through my mind, followed by an endless stream of questions. But before I could even ask who, what, or where I was, I was given the full details from a roomful of wide-eyed family members. One by one, they now came and hovered over me, some of them crying, while others began to recount my latest slice of dramatic pie.

"You died!" "Your lungs collapsed, and you flat-lined in the ambulance!" "They didn't think you'd live; and if you did, they said you'd be a vegetable!" One account after another kept coming at me as I continued staring at the hose next to my heart. According to the doctors, nurses, and everyone involved, it was a complete miracle that I was alive.

Needless to say, this experience was a total wake-up call. Since I'd left home at the age of 18, my health had never really been a priority to me. Occasionally I'd start an exercise program or run a few miles after watching one of my favorite *Rocky* movies, but that never lasted very long. And although I stayed fairly active by playing basketball during the summer months, my energy was short-lived due to my poor eating habits.

The biggest problem, though, was my mind. Stress and fear were the major reasons why I'd end up sucking on an asthma inhaler ten times a day. Whenever I felt the pressures of life crashing down on me, my lungs would quickly close up. Once in a while, I'd take one too many puffs on the inhaler and find myself passed out on my kitchen floor. My lack of health insurance kept me from receiving the care I needed, but more often than not it was my neurotic thinking that left me gasping for air—proving that the body truly is intimately connected to the mind.

More than a decade later, and 20 pounds lighter, I rarely experience any asthma symptoms, as each day now begins with me focusing on my health. Taking care of my mind (meditation), body (yoga and walking), and spirit (reading inspirational books) has completely transformed all areas of my life. I now breathe easier, feel happier, and am more energized in my 40s than I was at 16!

I've also learned that having a vibrant spirit is essential to a kinder existence. When we're sluggish due to poor eating habits, lack of physical activity, and sleep deprivation, the last thing we feel like doing is being kind. This is why self-care is so important if we want to have an open heart and mind. Simply put, the way we treat ourselves will determine how we treat others.

Abuse Takes Many Forms

Taking drugs and alcohol is, of course, a serious form of abuse. Living this lifestyle is unkind to both yourself and the world around you, and it assures you a one-way ticket to emotional and physical hell. This message is almost always woven into the presentations that I deliver to students. As I talk with them, stressing the importance of healthy living, I'm reminded of just how difficult it is to be a teenager today.

But perhaps even more damaging than the challenges of substance abuse and being bullied are the daily acts of unkindness that come in the form of verbal and psychological violence. Whether it's the pressure to fit in socially, wear a certain jeans size, or own the latest electronic device, the emotional cruelty our children are experiencing is at an all-time high. These daily stressors, combined with the desire to excel in academics and sports, are creating a culture of overmedicated teens.

And then there's the obesity crisis. It appears that comfort food has now surpassed drugs and alcohol as the most typical way kids deal with emotional pain. If you look at the statistics that are out there, you'll see that the same holds true for adults as well.

As destructive as physical neglect can be to your well-being, self-inflicted abuse in the form of unkind thoughts and words is far more dangerous. If you think of yourself as obese, ugly, or stupid—or tag yourself with any negative label—you're triggering harmful actions that stem from those beliefs. For example, if you're constantly calling yourself fat, you'll eventually *become* the characteristics of an overweight person. This will mean that overeating, not exercising, attempting to hide your body with larger clothing, and feeling insecure around thinner people will become habitual. The same is true if you brand yourself as *dumb* or *stupid.* By adding this description to your self-assessment, it's unlikely that you'll attempt anything that would potentially challenge your intelligence.

Unfortunately, I was a perfect example of this. For years I lived with a self-imposed identification of "I'm only a high-school graduate," which caused me to feel insecure around those who were more educated.

This limiting belief also ensured that I wouldn't attend my ten-year high school reunion. Even though I owned a successful photography business, I still felt "less than" when surrounded by individuals who had degrees. Today, however, I'm actually proud of the fact that I "only" have a high-school diploma. When I look at what I've been able to accomplish through perseverance and self-education, I feel a tremendous sense of confidence and pride.

The Heart's Perspective

Learning to fully accept who you are isn't something that typically happens overnight. It takes time for new habits to become solidified. With enough practice and a new perspective, self-abuse and disempowering labels can be transformed into confidence, vibrant health, and even self-love. So remember to be patient with yourself. Numerous studies have shown that after 21 days of repetitive behavior, a new pattern begins to develop. Positive addictions such as regular exercise, healthy eating, and even the ability to stop complaining, have been reported after a person sticks to a program for a full three weeks.

To create new wellness habits, start by accepting yourself exactly as you are today. No matter what your negative tendencies may be, it's important to fully embrace and treat yourself with love and kindness. For instance, if you're overweight, that doesn't mean you've failed or need to beat yourself up because of the extra pounds you're carrying. Acknowledging your current situation is a sign of strength, and it shows that you've found the courage to make positive changes in your life. Remember that resistance and denial are fear based and will only magnify the problem.

Ralph Waldo Emerson once said: "Self-trust is the first secret of success." By making the very first choice of being responsible or being a victim in Chapter 5, you've already established yourself as a responsible creator. Knowing that you're in control of your own life, you can now put your trust in your ability to lose weight, stop smoking, or eliminate self-defeating thoughts. Now is the time to take charge and create a life filled with vibrant, positive energy.

10 Ideas for Creating Wellness in Your Life

1. Using only positive, kind thoughts, make a list of the mental, physical, and spiritual aspects that you love about yourself.

2. Make time for spiritual practice each day through prayer or meditation.

3. Connect with nature. Walk; hike; swim; or simply immerse yourself in sunlight and fresh air, observing the magic of the natural world.

4. Breathe in and exhale the energy of gratitude. Give thanks every single day for the infinite blessings that surround you.

5. Laugh! Watch funny movies or spend time with energetic, humorous people.

6. Consider adopting a pet. Many studies reveal that animals can alleviate much of our daily stress.

7. Feed your mind with inspirational books and positive quotes.

8. Volunteer, serve, and make kindness your intention.

9. Choose high-grade "fuel" such as whole and organic foods. Also make water your number one drink.

10. Find an exercise program that *works for you,* and get moving. This one decision will transform your life.

Shifting Your Perspective

If you feel that you have any abusive tendencies, begin to change them right now. Shifting from a place of self-abuse to a place of wellness starts when you see your life as valuable—not only to yourself, but also to those around you. In other words, whenever you hurt yourself, you also hurt others.

When you see that improving your emotional and physical health is an opportunity to serve the people you care about, you become inspired to love yourself more fully. Take a deep breath and see yourself accepting your weight, addiction, or abusive habits while stating:

[Insert your negative habit] is an exciting opportunity for personal growth. Because of this challenge in my life, I now have the ability to elevate my mental, physical, and spiritual energy; boost my self-esteem; find personal freedom; and fully experience the joy of achieving my goals. I also know that by taking better care of myself, I can take better care of others.

Making the Choice

In the following paragraphs, there are portraits of two different people. One is habitually self-abusive, while the other lives a life of wellness. Each of these personalities experiences life differently. Read each description carefully, and then decide whether you're willing to choose wellness instead of abuse. Feel free to add any words that express your own feelings.

As a person who acts in self-abusive ways, I often feel: addicted, unhealthy, fat, lethargic, sick, depressed, weak, exhausted, powerless, or out of control.

I think others see me as: unhealthy, slow, over-weight, incapable, undisciplined, or hurting myself and everyone around me.

As a person who chooses wellness, I feel: ener-gized, sexy, attractive, strong, happy, fit, in control, admired, positive, inspired, emotionally and physically balanced, confident, self-loving, alive, kind, healthy, and respectful of myself.

I feel great every day and know that I am making a huge difference in the lives of others!

Questions for the Heart

Envision a time when you may have been abusive toward yourself or made poor health choices. How did this make you feel? Next, turn this emotion around by reflecting on the following questions. Then write down any thoughts or responses you have in your notebook or journal.

- What is wonderful about my mind, body, and spirit?

- How will living a healthier lifestyle benefit others?

- Am I being kind to myself and others by embracing this new perspective?

• • •

If you agree that a life of wellness is the kinder choice, complete the contract with yourself and sign your name.

I have chosen a life of wellness because I want to experience more _____

_____ *in my life.*

Your signature _____

Date _____

Choices now made: *responsibility, forgiveness,* and *wellness*

Consciously embracing wellness creates an environment in which positive energy thrives. You can put that energy to use as you make the next choice: to follow your dreams or settle for less.

• • •   • • •

Chapter 8

The Fourth Choice: Dream Big or Settle

We're all artists. Each of us arrived here with a fresh cosmic canvas, ready to express our unique gifts and talents and share them with the rest of the world.

This canvas was intended to be your very own extraordinary life. Included with it were the perfect brushes, a palette of colors, and everything you'd ever need to create a masterpiece. Each brush even had a special purpose. One would paint your career; another was for relationships; and others represented your passions, which would ultimately reveal your life's true purpose.

On the day of your birth, you were pure potentiality as the universe's intentions were placed flawlessly into your hands. Soon after you arrived, however, something very strange began to happen. Before you were even given a chance to use them, "art critics" began taking the brushes from your hands. This was very confusing for you, and you thought, *Why are they taking these away from me?* After all, you remembered having them even before you arrived here!

Soon, all your brushes were gone, and so was your once-pristine canvas. As each year passed by, parents, teachers, religious organizations, the media, and other well-meaning critics began to smear colors on your cosmic canvas that you *never* would have chosen. "No, no," these people said, "stay inside the lines. You'd be so much happier if you'd just paint (think and act) like me."

Sadly, over time the truth of who you are was becoming very unclear, as an unauthentic life began to take shape. The piece of art before you looked nothing like the one you were going to create. Your spirit and creative nature were taken from you and replaced with a belief system that made you feel confused and full of fear. Foreign concepts such as criticism, judgmental attitudes, prejudice, and insecurities were now everywhere.

Your canvas, once limitless and uniquely yours, now hangs on the wall as an unrecognizable portrait.

• • •

This scene is a sad depiction of most human lives. Although well intentioned, the various people that raise us from birth have unknowingly taken away our spiritual right of authentic self-expression. They, of course, don't realize the full extent of what they're doing because their actions are a result of *their* early "lessons."

Those who nurtured you surely did the best they could. So rather than live in the past or seethe with regret, you can make this a time to embrace new beginnings. Each person has a reset button in life that's readily available to be pushed. That button is called *today.*

Painting a New Picture

It makes no difference whether you're 9 or 90. Starting over becomes entirely possible when you have an awareness of who you truly are and what it is you'd like to create in your life. By rediscovering your original, unconditioned self, you can courageously take your current artwork off the wall and replace it with a fresh canvas. In a nutshell, in order to be authentically happy, you must reclaim your "brushes," follow your heart, and become the creator of your life once again.

Not long ago, I heard a disheartening piece of information that says it all: The majority of people in this country dislike their chosen profession. Each day, more than half of all U.S. citizens sit at their desks (or wherever they work) wishing that they could reverse time and completely start over. Of course, these statistics fluctuate with current conditions, but it remains clear that cries of "I wish I woulda" and "I shoulda" can be heard from the towers of corporate America all the way to the retail clerk at the mall—which is a sad situation indeed in the so-called land of opportunity.

Despite the character flaws I exhibited early in my life, this fourth choice actually came quite easily to me. Following my dreams was what tended to carry me through some of my more difficult times. Over the years I've learned to look at my heart as my own personal GPS for living an inspired life. I simply type in the address of my heart's desire and go! Sure, I may miss a street or two along the way, but it's only because I'm not paying attention.

The voice within will always get you to your destination. But you have to trust it . . . and yourself.

A Major Source of Unkindness

Another perhaps more obvious point is that those who despise their jobs bring their disgruntled energy into traffic, the grocery store, and, in many cases, home to their families. For most people, the daily grind of doing uninspiring work not only erodes their spirit, but can also breed random acts of unkindness.

I personally know this situation all too well. Night after night, I watched my father come home from work angry about something that had happened during the day. Sometimes doors being slammed were the clue, other times the dog's food bowl getting kicked like a football through the kitchen would let me know that it wasn't a good time to show him my report card.

Working 30-plus years for the railroad made him a hardened man and did absolutely nothing for his people skills. He hated his job, but it was secure and paid well. Besides, *his* father was not exactly the "follow your dreams, I believe in you, son" kind of guy. Dreams weren't encouraged or even spoken about in our family; a job was only a means to pay the bills—period. But for some reason, even when I was very young, the concept of just working for a paycheck made absolutely no sense to me. I loved to dream.

Why I felt this way and where it came from I'll never know, but one thing was certain: I loved to dream *big*.

My imagination was like a protective shield around me. Whenever things became difficult at home, I knew I could slip back into my mind and do or be anything I wanted. It always felt so safe in my dreams. I'd often imagine myself as a hero, wearing a cape and saving the world from perilous danger—a fantasy that, not surprisingly, still resonates deep within me. I also considered being a stuntman, NASCAR driver, DEA agent, movie director, and, in my darker days, a ninja assassin. Thankfully, I decided that Japan was a bit too far from home; and by the time I was 21, I traded in my Asian weaponry for a pocketful of film and a camera.

Dreams in Focus

From the first time I heard the shutter click on my 1970-something Minolta SR-T 101 camera, my heart grew ten sizes. I was completely in love, and I instantly began to imagine owning my own business one day and creating beautiful photography all over the world.

And as I previously mentioned, that dream of becoming a successful portrait photographer came true. I can honestly say that I didn't have a "job" during those years. Instead, I felt pure bliss whenever a camera was in my hand; and I never found myself looking at the clock, wanting to take breaks, or thinking about vacations. For me, photography was an incredible opportunity to express my creative spirit and meet hundreds of new people. It was an absolutely amazing time in my life, and it was all possible because of an accumulation of inspiring thoughts also known as . . . a dream.

Was it easy in the beginning? No. For many years I barely scraped by, worked odd jobs, borrowed money with credit cards (which I don't recommend), and lived in dumps just to keep my dream alive. But even though there were challenges along the way, I never found myself focusing on the struggles simply because . . . I was doing what I loved! Each day creative inspiration fed my soul and caused me to feel like the richest guy in the world, regardless of my empty refrigerator or gas tank.

The Next Big Dream

Soon after discovering the power of kindness, I knew that major changes were about to take place in my life. At the time of this epiphany, I was 16 years into my photography career, making good money, winning awards, traveling, and considered among the best in the portrait business (mostly ego stuff). So as you can imagine, when my wife and I told everyone that we were closing our studio and opening something called The Kindness Center, people thought we'd completely "lost it."

Even after explaining to everyone how I wanted to help others and change the world, I still received criticism for the decision to pursue this dream. I heard cries of "How will you pay your bills?" "Why would you completely close up your photography business?" and "How can you possibly make a career in *kindness?*"

Luckily, I've never really listened to the opinions of nondreamers. I've found that the critics are usually those who are dissatisfied with their own situations and have a difficult time with others who dare to pursue their desires. I knew with all my heart that this was the right thing to do, as if I'd been preparing for it my entire life. So with the unwavering support of my wife, who was also an award-winning photographer and co-owner of the business, we sold all of the photography equipment, closed the studio doors, and never looked back. And we've never regretted this decision.

Today, 20-plus years after shooting my first roll of film, I'm in the midst of a new dream and experiencing the most exciting time of my life. Each day I feel tremendous gratitude for all of the amazing things going on with The Kindness Center. It has truly been a remarkable period, and, despite the occasional challenges (and my temporary cut in pay), pursuing this vision has been the best thing I've ever done. By helping people change their lives, I'm helping to change the planet.

The Heart's Perspective

So what about *you?* What did you want to be growing up—a firefighter, a movie star, a boatbuilder, an artist, or a famous author? *More important, what do you want to do right now?* It makes no difference where you are today; if you have a dream in your heart, *you must express it.* You were born to share your desires with the world! This doesn't necessarily mean that you have to quit your day job or change your current situation, but if you don't reveal your enthusiasm to others, you may be in grave danger of never fully experiencing the joy of an inspired life.

Begin today by dusting off your childhood dreams, and you'll be amazed by how quickly your energy grows. Your imagination will make you feel ecstatic and alive! Expressing your unique passion is a tremendous gift that you give to yourself *and* those around you. Studies have shown that people who love what they do in life are typically happier and healthier, and treat others with more warmth and respect.

Close your eyes and see yourself doing something you have a passion for. Do you have the courage to turn this dream into a career? If so, go for it! But if you'd prefer to just live it on the weekends, that's okay, too. Whatever you do, don't allow your vision—whether ambitious or modest—to sit dormant any longer.

Here are some ideas for getting back into the flow of inspiration and realizing your dreams:

1. Do you have a burning desire to offer a service or product to the world? If your goal is to be your own boss, have creative control, and take long lunches, start putting your business plan together now!

2. If you once dreamed of being an actor or actress, rather than just being a member of the audience, join a theater group and audition for the roles that you want.

3. If you've always wanted to be a pilot, stop staring woefully at the sky—go online and find a local flight school.

4. If you've dreamed of being a writer, create an outline for a book and set aside time each week to write.

5. If you've ever fantasized about becoming a famous rock star, stop sitting in regret and listening to your mix tapes from the '80s. Go grab your craziest friend, find a karaoke bar, and belt out your favorite AC/DC songs.

Shifting Your Perspective

Many people claim to have no idea of what their true passion is. Perhaps the best way to discover yours is by answering one simple question that I once heard Cheryl Richardson ask in an audio program. Basically, she said: "If you were told that you could only visit one section of the bookstore for the rest of your life, what would it be?"

For example, if I were to answer this, my choice would obviously be personal growth/spirituality. Some people might say gardening; some will claim the travel section; while others may choose either cooking, fishing, music, or art. This simple question is a powerful clue to discovering what it is you truly love.

What would *your* response be? Take a moment now to ask yourself this question, and then answer the four that follow in your notebook or journal.

- Would you prefer to pursue your passion as a career or keep it as a hobby?

- What can you do today to make this dream a part of your life?

- How would you feel if you consistently expressed this desire?

- How would living this way benefit others?

Overcoming the Obstacles to Dreaming Big

I'll be the first to admit that dreaming big can be a bittersweet experience. I wish I could tell you that it's all rainbows and sunshine, but for most people, it isn't. The challenges that often accompany pursuing a passion are likely to create many obstacles, perhaps even heartbreak. As a matter of fact, at times they can cause you to feel like pure hell. But then again, so does settling.

When chasing any goal, it's important to accept the fact that, yes, there will be mountains to climb. But you also need to understand that these mountains are the most scenic (and transformational) part of your quest. Keep in mind that achieving your heart's desire will be a wonderful feeling, but the story of *how* you got there is even more profound. The truth is that when all is said and done, your experiences, personal resilience, and growth will give you the greatest sense of accomplishment. After all, as the saying goes, life is a journey, not a destination.

The reasons for not chasing a dream will be different for everyone. Some common excuses are "I'll get to it after I retire" and "I'll start when my kids are older." For some individuals, it's simply the dread of failure that holds them back. And, of course, the most typical justification for choosing a risk-free path relates to the fear of financial ruin. Sadly, money tends to be people's biggest excuse for not following their hearts.

First of all, let me say that these apprehensions are completely normal. Insecurity and, especially, uncertainty are part of the game. But they're also what make it such a blast! Life was meant to be an adventure, and greatness is rarely achieved without risk. Think about the paths of the brilliant leaders who continue to influence us today, such as Jesus; Gandhi; Abraham Lincoln; Martin Luther King, Jr.; and Mother Teresa. Their paths weren't what we'd consider easy! And take a look at the lives of some of our great visionaries: Walt Disney, Orville and Wilbur Wright, Thomas Edison, and Henry Ford. These individuals endured incredible hardships—often failing for years—yet through passion and persistence . . . *they changed the world.*

I'm not suggesting that you need to walk the earth promoting peace, or even come up with the next big invention. But I do feel that an inspired life leads to a kinder heart. When you have something that causes you to be creatively alive each day, you'll tend to radiate more happiness and treat the people around you a little better. I encourage you to start taking small steps toward something that ignites your spirit.

If you're already living your bliss, then this chapter can simply serve as a reminder to never settle in the future. However, if you aren't 100 percent satisfied with your particular situation, I'd like to offer you some tools of resiliency that you may find helpful. Personally speaking, the following ideas have been instrumental in helping me achieve both small goals and big dreams:

- Only share your intentions with people who are big dreamers. Closed-minded friends and family members will often give you reasons why something is impossible and unrealistic.

- Know that setbacks are blessings in disguise. When something doesn't work out, that's only the universe saying: "Be patient. I have something even better planned for you." This is the point at which vision, faith, and confidence are tested and often need to be reinforced.

- Only focus on what you *want* rather than what you don't want. If you focus on financial devastation, rejection, failure, or anything relating to lack, you'll only attract more of these negative thoughts. To manifest what you want, *focus on what you love* instead of what you fear.

- Keep your eyes on the prize, but remember to honor the journey. Not embracing the events along the way is like reading the last page of a great book first—all of the magic is lost and it robs you of the adventure. Enjoy every moment!

- Shift from *how* to *allow*. Once your work is done, simply let go of the *how* and let the universe do its thing. By allowing, you release all your worries and choose to trust in yourself/God/the universe.

- Remember that your dreams want you just as much as you want them. They're chasing you day and night. Notice moments of grace all around you. While on this path, you'll see signs of divine intervention everywhere. *These are not coincidences.* Everything that exists is here to serve and guide you.

- Use the mantra "Just one more day." When challenging times arise and you feel like giving up, say to yourself, "Okay, I'll give it just one more day." Repeat this as many times as necessary until you succeed.

Put no limits on your life! The time to start dreaming again is now. No more complaining. No more excuses. No more waiting. Rather than asserting, "I'm too old" or "It's too late," change your perspective and remember that you're a creative being and you can do *anything*. If you don't know what your first step should be, begin with your job. If you're currently in a career that you're unhappy with, there are two things you can do: (1) leave your job and do something that inspires you, or (2) change your attitude (perspective) about your current profession and look for opportunities to serve others with your unique gifts and talents.

Making the Choice

Portraits of two different people follow. One settles in life, while the other is willing to pursue a dream. Read each description carefully, and then choose which way of life seems more inspiring to you.

As a person who chooses to settle in life, I feel: bored, uninspired, unhappy, moody, too old, tired all the time, unappreciated, depressed, negative, helpless, powerless, underpaid, overworked, or disrespected by my boss.

It seems that I'm going to reach the end of my life with many regrets.

As a person who chooses to dream big, I feel: happy, inspired, kind, passionate, healthy, creatively alive, strong, vibrant, in control, admired, enthusiastic, as if I'm on cloud nine, positive, confident, cheerful, and excited.

I know that I'm: contributing to the world with my unique talents and fulfilling my heart's desire!

Questions for the Heart

Consider a time when you may have settled in your life. How did it make you feel? Next, turn this feeling around by reflecting on the following questions. Then write down any thoughts or responses you have in your notebook or journal.

- What would my life look like if I were inspired rather than tired each day?

- How could my goals and dreams have a positive effect on others?

- Am I being kind to myself and others by embracing this new perspective?

• • •

If you agree that having inspiring goals and dreaming big is the kinder choice, complete the contract with yourself and sign your name.

I have chosen to follow my dreams because I want to experience more _____

_____ *in my life.*

Your signature _____

Date _____

Choices now made: *responsibility, forgiveness, wellness,* and *dreaming big*

You've seen the obstacles to dreaming, learned about the cost of settling, and now realize the benefits of an inspired life. Choosing to discover and cultivate your passions is one of the greatest gifts you can give to yourself and the world. You're now ready for the next choice: creating a life of purpose or opting for one filled with indifference. This chapter will answer life's big questions: *Who am I?* and *Why am I here?*

• • • • • •

Chapter 9

The Fifth Choice: Living a Life of Purpose or a Life Without Meaning

---

Who am I? Since the beginning of time, this inquiry has troubled humanity perhaps more than any other. Typically asked during our later years, this riddle of existence can cause a lifelong search for our uniqueness and sense of purpose. Until my mid-30s, *Who am I?* was the burning question that I dealt with as I searched constantly for some clue of who or what I was. Strangely enough, the answer didn't arrive until I actually stopped looking. Giving up my attachment to needing an identity seemed to be the key to discovering a whole new aspect of myself.

Like so many of my enlightening moments, my own personal sense of self-realization was first discovered in a morning meditation. After a few minutes of focusing on my breath, I began to visualize a space in my mind's eye where I could contemplate some issues that had been weighing on me. I first imagined a simple room where I could sit in peace. While immersed in introspection, I was almost certain that this was the place where I'd discover the answers to what I'd been searching for: *Who am I, and what is my life really all about?* But as I flipped the light switch on in this mystical room, rather than revealing who I was, it revealed, with glowing clarity, *who I was not*. This was profoundly illuminating for me, and at the same time quite overwhelming.

The area was enormous—so huge that I couldn't see where it ended. Despite its vast dimensions, there was very little space to move around in. Cluttered with everything from material items, personal labels, and disempowering belief systems, it was an utter mess and desperately needed to be cleared out.

Standing there, I could see 30-plus years of accumulations and all of the things that once defined me. Everything was piled a mile high—awards, job titles, bank accounts, cars, past relationships, clothing, hairstyles, successes, failures, and even a blue ribbon for winning a push-up contest in the fourth grade. Based on my old theory that accumulation equals purpose, these were the things that I'd identified my existence with. I finally realized that letting go of this delusional belief system was the first step to understanding who I was and why I was here.

For months I returned to this same room through meditation, each time scrubbing and purging until I was finally able to see the walls and floors. Although it wasn't easy, truckloads of emotional debris had been removed and thrown into a cosmic Dumpster the size of the Grand Canyon. Hundreds, if not thousands, of negative labels and beliefs from "Depressed" and "Victim of a dysfunctional family" to "My father's suicide was my fault" had finally been destroyed through this visualization technique, each one tossed into a towering bonfire in my mind.

To my surprise, letting go of this old model of myself created an overwhelming sense of peace. My conscience had never felt lighter. While there were still a few items that I wasn't ready to throw away, I experienced the bliss of simplicity and personal freedom as each piece of waste was removed. Surely I'd have to "visit" this room again one day, but I was going to try my best not to go back for quite some time.

As I was finally leaving, I turned off the lights and closed the heavy metal door behind me. Turning to make sure it was locked, I noticed three faded letters on it: ego. There it was; I'd finally met the mental gremlin that had been responsible for most of my suffering.

The Heart's Perspective

Discarding your false self is the first step toward discovering your life's purpose. Once you fully understand who you *are not,* the truth of who you *are* will be revealed. Realizing that you're not your accumulations, accomplishments, or labels is a pathway to your true purpose and authentic happiness. This in no way implies that having material items or living abundantly is wrong. Experiencing financial security or owning possessions that bring you pleasure is a wonderful part of life. A family who buys a new boat can build a stronger bond by spending the weekends at a lake. A larger home with more space will accommodate guests more comfortably. A new car provides peace of mind on road trips. And more money allows someone to contribute to the charities that he or she feels passionately about.

Money, cars, homes, or any material item for that matter shouldn't be considered unspiritual. We all deserve to have tremendous abundance in our lives.

It's only when we become *attached* to this stuff that emotional danger lurks.

Thinking that you need these things in order to be happy is the source of your false identity and can cause a lifetime of fear and unhappiness. The ego wants you to remain addicted to the illusion that you are what you own, you are what you do (career or relationship), and you are your reputation. This phony self especially loves it when you seek approval and worry about the opinions of others. On the other hand, your spirit has no interest in any of that. By releasing yourself from the grip of your ego, you're reclaiming the life you were originally meant to live: to love, serve, and be happy.

Shifting Your Perspective

The most common misunderstanding individuals have is that their purpose comes in the form of a job title. Many people believe that being a teacher, nurse, or artist, for example, actually defines them. In reality, being an artist can be your *passion* in life, but it isn't your *purpose*. Your passions are simply the conduit you use to deliver your purpose. For example, a career in nursing will allow you to live out your true meaning, but the job itself is not your purpose. Artists can express their passion for Impressionism, but the title of "artist" isn't their reason for being.

Whatever our profession may be, I believe we all have the same purpose: *to be of service, make a positive contribution, and bring joy to the lives of others.* In a philosophical nutshell, enhancing the lives of the people around us in our own unique way is *the* reason for existing. Those who embrace this universal truth will always be on the pathway of true happiness and ease; those who don't may spend their entire lives searching for meaning.

Every time you improve another person's situation, you're at one with your purpose. One of the surest ways to do so is by aligning your passion with your mission. By living an inspired life, you'll discover the spiritual "fuel" that's necessary to contribute to the betterment of the world. This is why the fourth choice, *dream big,* is so crucial. By doing so, your energy allows you to positively influence the lives of others through whatever it is you believe in and love.

If you feel that your own life has no significance, it's likely that you're focusing more on receiving than giving. People who make it their daily intention to give and serve typically feel fulfilled and sleep quite well at night. This doesn't mean that you need to walk the streets feeding the homeless (although I highly recommend this activity) or travel to a developing country to help children in need. It's actually the small things you contribute each day that reveal your authentic meaning. This is what Mother Teresa meant when she said, "In this life we cannot do great things. We can only do small things with great love." In that spirit, the more you give and the more you love, the more you'll be in alignment with the very essence of your existence.

From Suffering to Service

Recently, a friend asked me to meet with a young man who was struggling with an addiction to drugs and alcohol. She'd been trying to help him for a long time, but nothing seemed to work. After I'd fully explained that I'm not qualified to counsel in the area of substance abuse, she still felt it would be beneficial for me to meet with him and share my thoughts on life. He and I arranged a time to get together at a local coffee shop, which is my preference when meeting new people, especially those who might be going through difficulties. A public place such as this one provides a safe environment, and it has plenty of private corners that are perfect for discussing matters of the heart.

When I first saw this guy, I had a difficult time believing that he could possibly be an addict. He looked so . . . well, normal. Right from the initial handshake, I knew I was going to like him. He was bright, good-looking, and talented; yet he felt that his life had no meaning whatsoever. He went on to talk about his past and how his drug use had begun at a very young age. He knew that abusing his mind and body like this wasn't right, but because he felt he had no real sense of worth, it became his way of escaping from the real world, and especially his feelings of loneliness.

As I listened intently for the next 30 minutes or so, I felt deep empathy for him. He was a good kid who'd simply made poor choices. He just needed someone to recognize what was *right* about his life rather than what was wrong. For me, this was easy. He had numerous positive qualities that just needed to be pointed out, one of which was his unique ability to "deliver" his purpose. Even before we met, I knew what he was meant to do. He, however, never saw it coming, and what I told him would ensure that he'd never look at his life in the same way again.

After letting the young man fully vent and share everything that he was willing to tell me, I looked straight into his hazy eyes and said: "What a wonderful gift this is to you and the lives of others."

Looking back at me, he didn't speak, but his expression said, "You're nuts."

I went on. "I'm serious. Your current struggles are a blessing, and you're going to be an inspiration to so many people." I continued, "Once you beat your addictions, and I *know* you will, you're going to have the opportunity to help others who are going through similar challenges. Your amazing story of courage will give hundreds, maybe thousands, of people hope! I can envision you speaking at schools or in front of groups focused on addiction recovery, sharing the message of how you were able to overcome these obstacles. Don't you see how important your life is? *You* will one day be changing the lives of others!"

His eyes were now gleaming, and he looked as if he were ten feet tall. "Wow," he said. "I never thought of it like that. That's an amazing way to think about it!" His body language now exuded confidence, and his newfound enthusiasm had replaced the uncertainty he'd been projecting just minutes before. Equipped with a totally new viewpoint, he went on to discuss ideas for serving others. He was no longer thinking about his own addictions, but rather how he could alleviate other people's pain. This huge shift literally came about in three minutes, and it took place simply because I had guided him to a heart-centered perspective.

The Blessing of Imperfections

There's a mistaken belief that in order to make a difference we need to be perfect or possess special talents. This is simply not true. Each of us is here for a reason and has something special to offer the world. The old fable that follows is a perfect illustration of this universal truth:

There was once a man in India whose duty was to fetch water for his master's house. He used two large pots, which hung on each end of a pole that he balanced on his neck. One of the pots was perfect and always delivered a full portion of water at the end of the long walk from the stream to the master's house. The other pot, however, had a crack in it and arrived only half full. For two years this went on, the man only able to deliver three-quarters of the amount he started with.

Of course, the perfect pot was proud of its accomplishments. But the poor cracked pot was ashamed of its imperfections and miserable that it was only able to accomplish half of what it had been created to do. One day by the stream, the cracked pot finally spoke to the water bearer about its perceived failure.

"I am so ashamed of myself, and I want to apologize to you."

"Why?" asked the young man. "What are you ashamed of?"

"For these past two years, I've only been able to deliver half of my load because this crack on my side causes water to leak out all the way back to your master's house. My flaw hasn't allowed you to get the full value for your efforts," the pot said.

The water bearer felt sorry for the cracked pot, and compassionately replied, "As we return to the master's house, I want you to notice the beautiful flowers along the path."

Indeed, as they went up the hill, the cracked pot took notice of the sun warming the beautiful wildflowers on its side of the trail, and this lightened its mood. But at the end of the walk, it still felt bad because it had once again leaked half its load. It apologized once more.

The man quickly responded: "Did you notice that there were flowers on your side of the path but not on the other? That's because I've always known about your flaw, and I took advantage of it. I planted flower seeds on your side, and every day while we walk back from the stream, you've watered them. For two years I've been able to pick these beautiful flowers to decorate my master's table. Without you being just the way you are, he wouldn't have this beauty to grace his house."

• • •

This sweet little story reminds us that despite being imperfect, we each have our own unique way of serving the world. An anonymous author once wrote: "Blessed are the cracked, for they shall let in the light." How true. We're all cracked pots. Whether we're letting in the light or spilling out water to help others grow, we're here for a reason, and the world needs us more than we could ever know.

Making the Choice

In the following paragraphs, there are portraits of two very different people. One demonstrates a life without meaning, while the other expresses true purpose. Read each description carefully, then decide which you'd like to experience.

As a person who finds little or no meaning in life, I spend a lot of time feeling: worthless, bored, unimportant, unhappy, uninspired, useless, unappreciated, insignificant, invisible to the world, or powerless.

I am afraid that I'll die not knowing what my life is all about.

As a person who lives a life of purpose, I feel: inspired, generous, loving, compassionate, significant, creative, passionate, happy, helpful, enthusiastic, confident, cheerful, excited, and kind.

I know I am: making a difference, changing people's lives, being a positive role model, and contributing to the world every single day!

Questions for the Heart

Recall a time when you felt that your life had no sense of purpose or meaning. How did that feel? Next, turn this feeling around by reflecting on the following questions. Then write down any thoughts or responses you have in your notebook or journal.

- What would my life look like if I knew that my sole purpose was to help others?

- How could this perspective impact the world?

- Am I being kind to myself and others by embracing this new perspective?

• • •

If you agree that a life of purpose is the kinder choice, complete the contract with yourself and sign your name.

I have chosen to live out my life's purpose because I want to experience more _____

_____ *in my life.*

Your signature _____

Date _____

Choices now made: *responsibility, forgiveness, wellness, dreaming big,* and *living a life of purpose*

In this chapter you've encountered the idea that you don't have to *search* for your purpose; it's really a matter of deciding *how* you will serve the world.

Now that you've made the choice to pursue a life of purpose, the next chapter will show you how to harness your energy and passion without letting toxic people and situations drag you down.

• • • • • •

Chapter 10

The Sixth Choice: Positive Relationships or Energy Vampires

It was honestly one of the most difficult things I've ever had to do. I'd never "broken up" with a guy before (and I wasn't sure if there was a manly way to do it), but what started out as an exchange of turbulent e-mails sadly ended with a phone call and a final good-bye to a friend who was once like a brother to me.

We both knew that it was only a matter of time; our relationship had become far too exhausting, and it was time to go our separate ways. He thought that

I was becoming "too deep and spiritual," while I felt that he was acting in ways that were insensitive and hurtful toward others. Being on a path of kindness, I was just so tired of talking about trivial stuff and, especially, making fun of people. At times I'd try to play along with his insensitive comments about others, but on the inside I felt dirty. I despised how I acted when I was with him. Each remark he made about overweight pedestrians—and his degrading jabs at women—made me cringe. Whether we were sitting in a restaurant or speaking on the phone, every interaction left me exhausted and pessimistic.

At heart, he really was a good person, but his unpredictable moods sapped my energy and made it difficult to be around him. One minute we'd be laughing and having a great time, and the next moment his temper would turn and he'd be trashing my "change the world" thoughts on life. Adding to the tension and awkwardness, his girlfriend was even telling him to stop being so negative when he was with me. I knew that something needed to be done—so yes, we broke up.

As difficult as it was, I can confidently say that letting go of this friendship improved my life and restored my spirit. Within days I felt lighter and more at peace than I had in a very long time. In fact, after a few weeks I was radiating so much joy that I actually began to attract positive individuals into my life. I went from having just a few friends to having hundreds of loving and supportive people around me. I'll admit that there were days when I missed my friend, but this reassuring new energy proved that I'd done the right thing for both of us.

With completely opposite worldviews, I was no better for this guy than he was for me. We needed to take different paths. From the bottom of my heart, I can honestly say that I hope he finds the same peace and good fortune that I have.

The Heart's Perspective

There is no denying that choosing the type of energy that surrounds you is vital to experiencing both happiness and kinder living. As author and motivational speaker Earl Nightingale famously said, "You become what you think about." The same can be said about the people you decide to spend your life with. The issue isn't just finding the right life partner or best friend; other choices matter, too. Your co-workers, the places you shop, and even the family members you associate with will determine whether you experience love and laughter or feel drained and depressed.

The idea is simple: by spending time with positive, happy people, you absorb their energy and become a positive, happy person yourself.

We all notice the individuals who light up a room with their optimism and love; and deep down, most of us secretly wish to possess these characteristics. They have energy that's contagious, and they're the ones who find a way to bring balance to a world that seems to be falling apart. Their sunny disposition and optimistic view of life are vital not only to having positive relationships, but also to saving the entire planet! They balance our universe by bringing light to the darkness.

The Tao of Mollie

To consistently experience positive relationships, we obviously need to be loving and kind. In learning to become a person with such desirable traits, I've often found that modeling our behavior after those who possess these qualities is extremely helpful. Not that we need to mimic someone's every move, but those who display heart-centered traits can truly be wonderful teachers.

My greatest teacher in the art of relationships is my friend Mollie. Her positive outlook on life,

wonderful sense of humor, and ability to love unconditionally inspire all who meet her. Although she's
only 6 years old, Mollie is still wiser than most people
who are 60—in fact, she's absolutely brilliant. She is
a divine spiritual teacher, my very best companion,
and . . . she's also a dog.

At 50 fluffy pounds, this four-legged sage has
taught me more about being a good husband, father,
and friend than anyone I've ever met. Her powerful
lessons are always with me as I communicate with
and relate to the humans I interact with each day.
Mollie teaches me lessons of *nonjudgment* (she accepts
everyone for who they are), *forgiveness* (she never
holds a grudge, even when scolded for stealing my
lunch off the counter), *humor* (she never takes herself or others too seriously), *enthusiasm* (she always
greets people with joy and excitement), *maintaining
an adventurous spirit* (she's always up for a ride, playing catch, or a late-night walk), and, the greatest
lesson of all: *unconditional love* (she doesn't know any
other way to live).

The truth is, Mollie doesn't care about my looks,
the kind of car I drive, my fashion sense, how educated I am, how much money is in my bank account,
or what I do for a living. She loves me no matter
what! Now that's what I call a *real* friend. And perhaps

if we all made it our intention to wag more and bark less, not only would our relationships thrive, but the world just might become a better place.

The Dark Side: Recognizing Energy Vampires

Good friends can be pretty easy for most of us to identify. An energy vampire, however, is a very different story. These are the people who have chosen to completely suck the joy out of life—and this *is* a choice, by the way, though perhaps not a completely conscious one. Unlike vampires in the traditional sense, these individuals aren't restricted to the nighttime, and they target happy people 24/7.

Whether it's at a family gathering or your place of work, these depressing creatures are continually looking for a source of energy, attention, or commiseration that they can latch onto. Sniffing out your happiness like warm blood, they'll sink their teeth into any opportunity to drain your life force by complaining about others, cutting down your dreams, or telling you how offended they are by the rest of the world. Their negativity can kill the human spirit.

Spending any amount of time with an energy vampire virtually guarantees emotional and physical exhaustion. Even worse, if you're not careful, they can infect you to the point that you actually become just like them. Yes, an energy vampire truly does *suck*. If you're uncertain whether or not you have one in your life, simply ask yourself the following questions:

- Do I feel anxious at work when certain people are near me?

- Do I feel uncomfortable or awkward around specific friends or family members?

- Do I feel depressed after speaking with certain people?

- Do I constantly get asked by anyone to "fix" his or her problems?

- Does anyone I'm around criticize me or others?

- Does someone in my life always complain about the weather, the economy, traffic, work, or his or her relationships?

If you answered *yes* to any of these questions, you most certainly have energy vampires in your life. Some examples of them may be:

- Negative co-workers

- Family members who constantly criticize you
- An egocentric boss
- Whiners and protesters
- Obnoxious neighbors
- Drama queens (and kings)
- Friends who complain about everything
- Unkind customer-service agents
- Closed-minded, perpetually angry, judgmental people
- Gossipers

These are just a few examples of those who can turn a really great day into a miserable one, if we let them. So how do we avoid these life-draining creatures? A garlic necklace? Wooden stakes? Holy water? Although these items would surely amuse other co-workers at the next company picnic, there *is* a better way to battle the dreaded energy vampire.

Shifting Your Perspective

The first thing you need to do is recognize who it is that's sucking the joy from your life. Yes, you will have to become a vampire hunter. Although this can be frightening to some people, it's an absolute necessity if you're to experience a kinder life. The good news is that you've been building up your immunity to them by making the positive choices you've learned about in the preceding chapters. This new way of living will create a shield around you and help to keep vampire fangs out of your life.

The second thing to be addressed (which is the most common argument with this sixth choice) is that we're stuck with certain people in our lives, and there's no way out. I understand that total avoidance may be difficult in family or work situations, but I also encourage you to keep in mind that you choose the amount of time spent with these individuals. For example, during the holiday season, which is filled with countless gatherings, it's inevitable that there will be a relative who can be draining to be around. Almost every family has at least one energy vampire who talks incessantly about others and loves to gossip.

So what do you do? Do you stand there listening, becoming emotionally depleted? Or do you excuse yourself from the conversation and find more positive people to be around? There's also the choice of agreeing with the attacker or not, which reinforces his or her behavior. Instead, you can decide to say something kind about the individual who's being criticized. You *always* have a choice.

Although there are some situations where we can (and actually should) cut extremely negative people from our lives, the reality is that we need to learn to get along with each other. One way to do so is to bring love and kindness into the presence of energy vampires. This has the power to nullify their negativity, and over time it can actually convert their darkness into light. Shining kindness on these gloomy souls is like driving a stake through their hearts. Instead of destroying them, though, this much-needed jolt is often a wake-up call to a kinder way of life.

Is it easy to react with kindness to an energy vampire? Not always. But this is perhaps our best option for both personal and global survival. If we don't learn to send love to the grouchy, complaining "you-know-whats," I fear we may be in big trouble.

Their unkind ways will continue to infect the rest of the world, causing a global epidemic.

Other Energy Drains

Sometimes it's not just people who consume our spirit. Uninspiring jobs, our environment, clutter, unfinished tasks, and unfulfilled commitments can all leave us feeling depleted and, sometimes, defeated. When that happens, we have little desire to attract and engage in fulfilling relationships.

The focus of this chapter is identifying the energy-draining people in your life; and instead choosing positive, healthy connections. It's worth your while, however, to spend a few minutes thinking about all of the other aspects of your life that have this effect on you and make a plan to manage them, too.

Making the Choice

Here again are portraits of two extremely different people. One allows energy vampires to dictate their emotions, while the other chooses to be surrounded by uplifting people and positive energy. Each one leads to different life experiences. Read each description carefully, and decide what you'd like your experience to be.

As a person who chooses to allow energy vampires in my life, I feel: exhausted, unhappy, drained, weary, disrespected, depressed, powerless, or worn out.

I find that I am: shunned by positive people, allowing others to control my feelings, and experiencing a life filled with drama.

As a person who chooses true friends and positive relationships, I feel: strong, loving, compassionate, generous, happy, vigorous, admired, confident, and passionate.

I find that I am: having fun, surrounded by positive people, and contributing to the lives of others with my vibrant energy!

Questions for the Heart

Bring to mind an energy vampire in your life. How does it feel to be surrounded by his or her negativity? Next, turn this feeling around by answering the following questions to help you decide how to handle this situation. Then write down any thoughts or responses you have in your notebook or journal.

- Can I convert this negativity into love and kindness? How?

- Do I need to end this relationship in a peaceful way, wish this person well, and move on with my life? What's the best way to do so?

- Am I being kind to myself and others by changing the way I think about this person, even if I have to end the relationship?

• • •

If you agree that surrounding yourself with positive people is the kinder choice, complete the contract with yourself and sign your name.

I have chosen to develop positive relationships because
I want to experience more _____
_____ *in my life.*

Your signature _____
Date _____

Choices now made: *responsibility, forgiveness, wellness, dreaming big, living a life of purpose,* and *positive relationships*

You have seen the destructive effect that energy vampires (whether human or inanimate) can have on the life you desire, and you have chosen positive energy and relationships instead. Next, you'll see that all of the information from the rest of Part II has led you to this final decision, one that ultimately has the power to bring happiness to yourself and others: choosing a life of *kindness* or *unkindness.*

• • •   • • •

Chapter 11

The Seventh Choice: A Life of Kindness . . . or Unkindness

It was Monday, it was snowing again, and to be honest, I was about to lose my mind. My impatience with Maine winters had finally peaked, as just about every other day we were digging ourselves out of a snowstorm. This was also the fourth straight Monday that we'd been hit, and I was sick and tired of it.

I had tons of office work to do that morning, and being stuck outside with the snowblower and shovel wasn't inspiring me to be very kind. In reality, I was acting like a complete jerk, and my expletives toward

Mother Nature surely had my neighbors wondering how in the world I had ever come to be called The Kindness Guy. To make matters worse, with each pass of the snowblower, it would clog up and stall due to the wall of packed snow the city plow had left me at the end of my driveway.

I was wet. I was cold. And I was completely infuriated with winter.

An hour and a half later, I'd finished the driveway, but I knew my despondent mood would get me nowhere if I didn't make a major shift. I also knew exactly what I needed to do to change my attitude—it was just a matter of making myself do it. Realizing that I'd be no good to myself or anyone else in this state, I went to the front door and asked Cara for the keys to my truck. Seeing my murky energy, she asked me with concern, "Are you going somewhere?"

"Yes," I abruptly replied.

"Where?"

"I have to go do something before I completely lose it," I said.

My wife understood exactly what this meant. After saying good-bye to her, I loaded the snowblower into my truck, grabbed a shovel, and headed into town. After driving around for about ten minutes, I saw my first target: a 70ish-looking woman who was throwing heavy slush over her shoulder. Without hesitation, I quickly parked the truck on the street, jumped out (willing myself to smile), and cheerfully told the woman, "Good morning! I'm out doing random acts of kindness and would love to clear your driveway for you—for free!"

At first she looked at me as if I were green and had antennae coming out of my soggy winter hat. But after telling her that I was from The Kindness Center and it was something we loved to do, her eyes began to sparkle with immense gratitude. She didn't know if I was for real, but she was grinning from ear to ear.

And that was all I needed. It only took one look at her beaming face . . . and I was a goner. She'd killed my bad mood and brought me back to life through a heart-to-heart resuscitation.

For the next few hours, I was in pure ecstasy as I cleared driveways for complete strangers. Despite being exhausted and frozen to the bone, I was now smiling, laughing, making new friends . . . and absolutely in love with winter! I was even making plans for the next storm and wondering why I'd ever disliked snow so much in the first place! It's amazing how the things we dislike become pure joy when we're doing the same activity for someone else.

This method has proven to be my saving grace more times than I can even begin to count. Performing spontaneous acts of kindness has become my guaranteed way of getting out of bad energy and into a natural state of joy. It has also proven to me that service truly does dissolve suffering.

The Heart's Perspective

The pathway to happiness really is that simple. No pills, no therapy, no looking into the mirror and repeating affirmations for a lifetime—all we need to do is *be kind*. Science has shown how an act of kindness is so powerful that it actually alters our brain chemistry. According to research that has been widely cited in recent years, kindness increases our levels of serotonin—a hormone that allows us to feel light, happy, and at ease—and even strengthens our immune systems. This, of course, is the purpose of antidepressants, which were designed to increase the production of this happy chemical in our brains.

Studies have also revealed that a single act of kindness not only escalates the levels of serotonin in the person performing the kind deed, but also in the recipient. What's even more astonishing is this: Those who are simply *observing* an act of compassion or generosity are affected in the same way! The giver, the receiver, and the witness *all* exhibit an increase in serotonin. Could it be that we've discovered a cure for sadness and mild depression?

Consider what this says about the nature of human beings. If our bodies and minds are in harmony when we're being kind, doesn't it make sense that this should be our natural way of communicating? It's clear that kindness leads to inner peace; therefore, by extension it must be our pathway to world peace as well.

Everything you've been working on in the previous chapters has led you to the definitive and transformative decision to be kind. Assuming that you've already made the empowering choices in the previous six chapters, you can be assured that by choosing a life of kindness your world will never be the same again. By adopting this new lifestyle, you're also adopting a totally different set of principles. While they may be challenging at times, they'll ultimately lead you to a life filled with meaning.

Shifting Your Perspective

When I began my own journey of kindness, I had no idea just how powerful living from my heart could be. Sure, I thought it might help me to be a better husband, father, and friend; but never in my wildest dreams did I believe that it would become a conscious part of everything I do. To be honest, at one time the word *kindness* only seemed like a way of being extra nice from time to time. So the idea of actually making it a lifestyle (and then teaching it) almost seemed impossible.

But over time, and after months of research, I started to notice something very profound. I discovered that there are three simple things we can do to shift from suffering to pure joy:

1. **Think** kind thoughts about yourself and others.

2. **Speak** kind words about yourself and others.

3. **Act** in kind ways toward yourself and others.

I found this magic formula to be the antidote to depression, fear, anxiety, anger, hatred, resentment, being judgmental, and all other negative emotions. If this seems unrealistic, try it for yourself. Try to think, speak, or act in a kind manner and feel bad in that same moment. If you can accomplish this, I daresay that you're not from this planet. I've yet to find one person who can radiate the energy of kindness while experiencing misery simultaneously.

Through this discovery, I also began to see how practicing this way of life actually reveals our most beautiful qualities—such as patience, compassion, courage, and authenticity, just to name a few. Even more fascinating was the realization that these are the characteristics of the happiest and most peaceful people I know. After additional research (and personally testing *every* theory), it was soon obvious to me that kindness is more than just being nice; rather, it's the vehicle for delivering unconditional love. I fully understood that, at its very essence, *kindness is the creative distribution of love.*

To be creative with your heart is your greatest gift to the world. There's simply no greater offering than to share this energy with those around you. Intentional kindness will forever change the way you communicate in your relationships and daily interactions.

But perhaps even more powerful is the experience of connecting with individuals you don't know—yes, complete strangers. Understandably, this isn't easy for most people, especially since at a very early age you were probably taught not to talk to strangers and to stay out of dark alleys.

We do need to be safe and make intelligent choices when potential danger is near, but when a man is simply standing beside us in a coffee shop, why is it that we can't even acknowledge his existence? Why can't we make eye contact? Why can't we smile and say, "Hello. I'm out performing spontaneous acts of kindness today, and I'd love to pay for your coffee!"

There's no doubt that reaching out to a stranger may cause feelings of insecurity and fear. I have done this hundreds of times and still get the jitters. But with time, and by applying the ideas in the upcoming chapters, you'll find the courage to practice one of life's greatest highs: *performing spontaneous acts of kindness.*

Anchors: The Obstacles to a Life of Kindness

So what about everyday life? Why is it so difficult for some people to express warmth in a work setting, or even in their own home? I've discovered that those who have a difficult time adopting a lifestyle of kindness have many of the same characteristics, most of which relate to the insensitive qualities of the ego. I call these *anchors,* which are the heavy emotions or attitudes that keep us from moving forward in life. Unfortunately, many of us drag our emotional anchors around for a lifetime. What follows are some of the most common traits of individuals who choose an unkind life. In addition to acting like a victim, being resentful and abusive, settling, living a life without purpose, and choosing negative relationships, they also . . .

- . . . are extremely defensive and love to argue.

- . . . crave approval or need to be liked by everyone.

- . . . are ungrateful.

- . . . are difficult to work with.

- . . . constantly get offended.

- . . . are impatient.

- . . . believe that they are superior to others.

- . . . love to gossip.

- . . . only talk about themselves.

- . . . take life too seriously.

- . . . make everything a competition.

- . . . always need to be right and make others wrong.

Looking at the makeup of such a person can be a real wake-up call. It sure was for me. I'm the first to admit that at one time I had nearly all of those less-than-kind qualities. I also had absolutely no idea that this was the energy I was projecting to the world. Occasionally I'd get called out on my pessimism, but my head was too thick to fully understand that I was being more than just negative, I was being completely unkind.

Most of us have been taught that there are two ways of thinking: positively and negatively. I've discovered that a powerful new way to look at these two labels is to see them as *kind* or *unkind*. For example, rather than saying *positive thinking,* I replace the word *positive* with *kind*. Or, if I catch myself thinking optimistic thoughts, I simply notice this as *kind thinking*. (I also call this having a *kind mind*.) The same is true for *negative*. Instead of referring to someone as having *negative energy,* I see this as *unkind energy*. This has been a very effective tool for creating a kindness consciousness in my daily life.

A New Way of Living

You've now completed Part II of this book, which has revealed critical choices that undeniably create a happier and kinder life. But you won't be signing the last contract just yet. Before committing to this definitive seventh choice: *a life of kindness or unkindness,* you'll have the opportunity in Part III to see what is involved in living this way.

• • • • • •

part iii

Livingkindness: Kindness as a Way of Life

Chapter 12

The 5 Keys to Kindness

The 5 Keys to Kindness are your gateway to authentically living and nurturing each of your seven choices. The power of each key lies in its simplicity. Unlike some personal-development teachings that add to life's complexity, these were created to actually make life *easier*. They are principles of the heart that reveal how happiness was truly meant to be an effortless state of being.

The 5 keys are:

1. *Being aware* of thoughts, words, and actions

2. *Asking* "am I being kind"

3. *Adopting* the Livingkindness philosophy

4. *Applying* the 9 Elements of a Kind Heart

5. *Performing* acts of kindness

Being Aware

*Become mindful of your thoughts,
words, and actions.*

To embrace a life of kindness, we must first become conscious of our daily thoughts, words, and actions. Also known in Buddhist philosophy as *mindfulness,* being aware of how we relate to the world around us is absolutely vital to kinder living. By learning to recognize our own behavior, we can take control of our personal energy rather than walking unconsciously through life and hurting those around us.

In most cases, people who act in unkind ways aren't even aware that they're being insensitive. How often do we see oblivious co-workers leaving a trail of misery throughout the office, only to arrive at their desks with no sense of remorse or understanding of the effect they've had? What about the angry driver, red-faced and filled with rage, blowing his horn at the first sign of heavy traffic? Or perhaps it's a family member who's constantly griping about others. Do they really know what they're doing? Are they out to destroy the world? Is their mission in life to be a complete jerk? I don't think so.

Unconscious behavior is the number one factor in unkind living. I believe, at heart, that all people were born with only loving qualities, and it's through our human conditioning that we act in callous and unfeeling ways. Therefore, to make kindness our primary way of life, we must become *aware* of and return to our true nature.

One of the surest methods to reconnect with your original self and become the observer of your life is by quieting your mind through meditation. The simple practice of closing your eyes and focusing on your breath, even for five minutes a day, can allow you to generate more clarity and inner peace.

Meditation is to the mind what showering is to the body. If you didn't wash yourself from Monday to Friday, by Saturday you'd be covered in five days' worth of dirt, sweat, and air toxins. This is exactly what happens to your head. After multiple days of worry, anger, and literally thousands of stressful thoughts, your mind becomes polluted and can't operate with clarity and loving intentions. By taking the time to be in silence each day, you're able to clear out the emotional clutter, which will mentally, physically, and spiritually restore you.

Below are a few techniques for becoming more aware of your thoughts and actions. Each method will help you be at ease while opening your heart to more compassionate living.

- **Meditate, pray, or choose to spend time in silence each day.** Even setting aside just a few minutes per day can recharge your spirit and give you a greater sense of clarity.

- **Connect with nature.** Take a walk, explore the woods, or spend time near a body of water. These activities can be wonderful forms of meditation.

- **Simplify your life.** Remove excess stuff, clean out your closets, and donate items that are no longer being used. Physical clutter is often linked to unconscious mental anxiety and stress.

- **Slow down.** Hurried behavior and impatience disconnect you from clear thinking and recognizing the needs of others. To offer your kindness to the world, slow your pace.

Asking

*Ask yourself throughout each day,
"am I being kind?"*

Asking "am I being kind?" is the ultimate tool for creating awareness. The next time you're about to argue, complain, consume unhealthy food, yell at a loved one, or even litter, take a deep breath and inquire within: "am I being kind?" By pausing and internally posing this question, you will not only become more aware, you'll begin to make kindness toward yourself and all of life a daily practice.

If you're unsure when to apply this powerful phrase, a simple rule of thumb is to look at it from another perspective and consider, "Would I want my children to act this way?" Gandhi famously said, "You must be the change you wish to see in the world." Perhaps this could be slightly revised: we must be the change we wish to see in our children. If you don't have kids, you can simply reflect on how you'd like others to treat you in a similar situation. How often have we heard mothers and fathers tell their children, "It's not nice to gossip and talk about other people," while they're habitually performing this act of unkindness around their family and friends? Many times, adults preach good manners and politeness while behaving in ways that are incongruent with their own rules.

My good friend Tom always says, "Whenever I make a decision with kindness, I always seem to make the right choice." My brother-in-law Mike often follows "am I being kind" with, "What's the kindest possible thing I can do in this moment?" Personally, I find both of those outlooks valuable.

"am I being kind" is the perfect inner mantra whenever you feel anxious, angry, or conflicted; or if you simply need to make the right choice. When you take a deep breath and reflect on this question before reacting in any situation, you'll find that it's the key to both inner and outer peace. And opportunities to use this inquiry of the heart will pop up everywhere. Here are a few to consider:

- You've just finished a healthy meal when someone offers you a triple-fudge brownie the size of a brick. You graciously accept it even though you're trying to lose ten pounds. Before you take a bite, pause, take a deep breath, and ask yourself, "am I being kind to my body?" What do you do?

- While in a hurry to pick up a few groceries after work, you see an opportunity to cut

into a parking space ahead of someone
who was obviously heading right for it.
Just before you pull in, pause, take a deep
breath, and ask yourself, "am I being kind
to this person?" What do you do?

- While out for an evening walk, you
  notice litter in the street in front of your
  neighbor's home. You decide to ignore it
  because it's not your problem. But before
  walking any farther, pause, take a deep
  breath, and ask yourself, "am I being kind
  to the earth and my neighbor?" What do
  you do?

- A co-worker who drives you crazy inspires
  you to make a rude comment that will
  get big laughs from others in the office,
  but likely hurt this person's feelings. Just
  before you speak, pause, take a deep breath,
  and ask yourself, "am I being kind to my
  co-worker?" What do you do?

- You're about to honk your horn and yell at
  a woman who accidentally cuts you off in
  traffic, and you notice that she's driving a
  carful of kids. Before exploding with anger,
  pause, take a deep breath, and ask yourself,

"am I being kind to this family?" What do you do?

- Earlier in the week, you promised your spouse that you two would spend Friday evening together having dinner and watching a movie. But Friday morning you get an offer to go out for drinks with some friends after work. You decide that your significant other will probably understand, and the two of you can go out next week. But before you call to let your significant other know about your change of plans, pause, take a deep breath, and ask yourself, "am I being kind to my husband/wife?" What do you do?

As you can see, this simple question is the ideal personal device for creating awareness, and it can also help you make choices that benefit yourself and those around you. Each time you ask this question, you can follow up by inquiring, "How may I be kind?" From there, your only job is to listen and then act in a way that's congruent with your heart. Using this technique throughout your day is a powerful method for transitioning into the third key: *Livingkindness*.

Adopting

Adopt the Livingkindness philosophy by practicing kindness toward yourself, others, and the earth.

The Dalai Lama once said, "My religion is very simple. My religion is kindness." What a simple yet profound creed! Having adopted this same philosophy, I've discovered that this belief system supports not only my own spiritual journey, but more important, *all of life.*

Unlike some religions that reject people for a variety of unkind reasons, the doctrine of unconditional kindness leaves no room for judgment or exclusion. No person, creature, or part of this planet is left out. As a way of life and our daily intention, this commitment becomes our greatest vehicle for consistently experiencing happiness and the energy of love. Created as just one word (because *living* and *kindness* shouldn't be separate), Livingkindness has three main principles for establishing a heart-centered life. By adopting each one, you'll notice positive changes in yourself and everyone around you.

The three principles are:

1. **Kindness toward yourself.** Self-kindness means nourishing your life with healthy

food, exercise, laughter, a career you love,
and personal and spiritual growth. It also
means making room in your schedule for
activities that inspire you, spending some
time alone in silence, and always choosing
kind thoughts about yourself.

2. **Kindness toward others.** You'll encounter
    dozens of opportunities each day to be kind
    to others. Practice kindness toward your
    family, friends, co-workers, and even strang-
    ers. Speak kind words about people, be a
    good listener, smile often, and give sincere
    compliments.

3. **Kindness toward the earth.** Make time
    each day to be kind to the earth. This prac-
    tice starts with simple things that you may
    already be doing. Ride your bike or walk
    (rather than drive), recycle, pick up trash,
    purchase environmentally friendly prod-
    ucts, and be compassionate toward animals
    and all living things.

By referring back to the second key and asking, "am I being kind toward others, the earth, and
myself?" you'll find it possible to stay on a genuine

path of kinder living. There will be days when it's difficult to adhere to this philosophy, to say the least. Existing in a world that often feels complex and stressful, most people simply can't sustain this practice 100 percent of the time.

Know that you don't need to become perfect or act like a programmed "kindness robot"; a much more achievable goal is to *change your kindness-to-unkindness ratio.* For example, if you feel that you maintain a kind lifestyle only half the time, consider new ways to live benevolently 70 percent of your day. A 70/30 ratio is a powerful step toward changing the consciousness of this planet. Just imagine if all people were at 70 or 80 percent! This collective energy would undoubtedly cause the negativity on the planet to implode.

To believe in the possibility that you could consistently live at 90 or 100 percent is quite unrealistic and will ultimately only lead to frustration. Go easy on yourself. If you feel that you're currently living 30 percent from your heart and 70 percent from your head, and tomorrow you increase to 31 percent from your heart, that's wonderful! Your only goal should be to improve and move forward each day. Of course, the more you grow, the happier and more at peace you'll become; but it doesn't benefit you to spend time judging or, especially, comparing yourself to those around you. Just make it your intention each day to consciously do a little more for others, and watch how quickly your life begins to change.

Applying

Apply the 9 Elements of a Kind Heart.

Perhaps our best-known teachings at The Kindness Center are the 9 Elements of a Kind Heart. These 9 components have been instrumental in teaching at schools, talking to businesses, and working with individuals. Each one reveals what kindness truly looks like when it's broken down into specific qualities and applied to our daily lives. Students have used these elements to become kinder in the classroom, while employees have discovered their power in both customer and co-worker relations. Each one can be likened to a piece of a heart-shaped puzzle; when only a few of the pieces are put together, it appears fragmented, with many empty spaces. But when the puzzle is completed, the heart is vibrant and fully alive!

By applying the 9 Elements of a Kind Heart to everything you do, you'll discover the secret to communicating with love and inviting endless blessings into your life. These elements, which are so instrumental to living a life of kindness, will be described in more detail in the next chapter.

A kind heart is . . .

- . . . *Attentive.* An attentive heart recognizes the needs of others.

- . . . *Authentic.* An authentic heart is genuine and acts from truth.

- . . . *Charitable.* A charitable heart gives yet expects nothing in return.

- . . . *Compassionate.* A compassionate heart is sensitive toward all living things.

- . . . *Courageous.* A courageous heart acts from love rather than fear.

- . . . *Enthusiastic.* An enthusiastic heart displays limitless energy and passion.

- . . . *Grateful.* A grateful heart is content and filled with appreciation.

- . . . *Inspirational.* An inspirational heart encourages and motivates others.

- . . . *Patient.* A patient heart waits and responds at the proper moment.

Performing

Perform spontaneous acts of kindness.

I had dubbed the event "24 Hours of Kindness." The goal was simple: to perform as many acts of kindness as possible in the community for a full 24 hours without sleep. Thanks to our local radio station, Coast 93.1, all of southern Maine knew about our crazy event. As I've said, I was now known as The Kindness Guy, and this was my first attempt at something this big. The local—and even national—media buzz was incredible.

Since 9:00 that morning, two of my kindness cronies and I had been all over town delivering free baked goods to nursing homes and schools, buying coffee for strangers, giving out hugs, moving furniture, passing out free bus fare, and completely flooding the town with a rainbow of flowers and balloons. Since it was April 15, tax day, we even spent time making grouchy taxpayers smile as they rushed in and out of the post office (a task we repeated later that night with miraculous results).

At 5 P.M., still with 16 hours to go, my adrenaline showed no signs of waning. After handing out a few more flowers and offering up free hugs at the grocery store, we were on our way to the local soup kitchen before heading to the next city for the remainder of the night.

Arriving at dinnertime, we walked though a sea of hungry souls waiting to get inside for their final meal of the day. As I looked into the eyes of the children standing in line, my upbeat energy quickly softened, and what I saw brought me down to earth. Until this point, we'd spent our time making people laugh and smile with our kind deeds, but this stop was very different. Standing there seeing the tattered clothing and leathery faces, I felt my heart breaking. I couldn't help but feel enormously grateful that I had a warm home and was blessed with all of the necessities in life. This also prompted a slight sense of guilt.

Walking into the kitchen, we found volunteers busily preparing salads, desserts, and gallons of iced tea. People were now filtering into the dining area, and the room began to buzz. The main dish would be ready soon, and we'd have an opportunity to deliver the meals. Looking around, I became inspired with an idea to brighten up the room.

Local florists had donated hundreds of carnations to our 24-hour mission, and we still had dozens of them in the truck. Passing them out seemed like a wonderful opportunity to bring smiles to the faces of the women and children now sitting at the tables, and the result was absolute magic. With each carnation offered, eyes sparkled with excitement and gratitude. I joyfully bounced from table to table receiving everything from soft grins, laughter, occasional hugs . . . and even tears.

After handing out most of the flowers, I walked toward the back of the room where I noticed a woman sitting alone, appearing quite worn down. Unlike many of the others there, she continued making direct eye contact with me until we were finally face-to-face. Smiling, I extended my hand and offered her one of my remaining white carnations. She looked confused and overwhelmed by my gesture. Slowly opening her hand, she accepted the flower with a bowed head as tears began to form in her eyes. Hoping that she was okay (or that I hadn't upset her), I quietly asked if she was all right. Seeming somewhat embarrassed, she lifted her head and stared up at me, now with tears streaming down her cheeks. She said, "This is just so nice . . . and, well . . . I haven't received a flower from anyone in over ten years."

I immediately felt a large lump form in my throat as moisture settled in my own eyes and impaired my vision. I knew that I was about to "lose it" at any moment, and there was only one thing left to do: dropping the remaining flowers from my hand, I bent down, wrapped my arms around this woman, and hugged her as tightly as I could.

Shortly after dinner, my kindness crew and I quietly shuffled out the back door to prepare for our night in the city. The next 14 hours were filled with everything from feeding homeless people, delivering coffee and bagels to police stations, mopping floors at a food pantry, and even bringing peace to an angry crowd of last-minute taxpayers who were attempting to get their envelopes to the post office before midnight. It was an absolutely crazy day.

Although both my body and my mind were completely shot by the time our 24th hour rolled around, I can honestly say that my spirit was ready to do it all over again. Next to my wedding day and the birth of my son, it was without a doubt the greatest day of my life.

It's been a few years since the first 24 Hours of Kindness. We've since held other kindness events, and I haven't fully come down from the highs that each one created. But after performing hundreds of kind acts, giving multiple interviews to the media, and sharing this experience with thousands of people around the country, my heart always goes back to the grace of the sweet little lady holding a single white carnation each time I think about that day. What a wonderful reminder that it truly is the simple things in life that mean the most.

• • •

Welcome to the magical world of performing spontaneous acts of kindness! Stories based on the hundreds of deeds performed during our events would easily fill more pages than this book could hold. Some are simple, quiet exchanges of the heart, while others will no doubt affect me for a lifetime. But you don't need to get out on the streets for 24 hours to change someone's life. There are dozens of opportunities around you every single day.

Seneca, the Roman philosopher and statesman, said it best: "Wherever there is a human being, there is an opportunity for kindness." So unless you live on a deserted island, there's really no excuse! Every day you'll be given the chance to make someone smile or feel loved or give a sense of hope. The question is: will you choose to act or not? I believe that if you've read this far, you've already made the decision to live a kinder life, and you now have the courage to *act*.

• • •

The chapter you've just completed contains quite a bit of information. To make it easier to absorb the material, you might find it useful to, in your own words, capture the essence of the 5 Keys to Kindness and the three basic principles of Livingkindness (kindness toward yourself, others, and the earth) in your notebook or journal.

The 9 Elements of a Kind Heart, which were mentioned briefly in this chapter, are discussed in more detail next.

• • •   • • •

Chapter 13

The 9 Elements of a Kind Heart

As I introduced in the previous chapter, the 9 Elements of a Kind Heart are tools you can use to create the life you desire. In addition to being a positive method for communicating, these 9 elements are also helpful in performing spontaneous acts of kindness.

As you look over the 9 elements, you'll notice that each one is an act of kindness itself, while also being a way to deliver a loving deed. Consider how you may use these elements to reach out to people you know . . . or even those you don't know. Applying all of them will assuredly change the way you interact with the world. But remember, *application* is the key here. These tools were created for active use and not merely as an interesting new theory. As the saying goes, love isn't love until you give it away. The same is true of these pieces of your heart. Begin giving them away today. . . .

Attentiveness

An attentive heart recognizes the needs of others.

To be attentive and notice when someone could use a helping hand or kind word takes us back to the first key to kindness: *being aware.* If we are to make a difference in the lives of others, we must become conscious and open our spiritual eyes. Having an attentive heart can be as simple as noticing a pedestrian trying to cross the street or seeing a neighbor struggling with groceries. Using our radar and continually scanning for those who require our assistance gives us countless opportunities to be kind. However, with so much need in the world, it's necessary to create boundaries and know our limits—it's unrealistic to think that we can help every single person on our path. But if we can heighten our instinctive heart-sense a little more each day, not only will we become more aware of what we can do for others, we'll also experience one of life's greatest gifts: the joy of service.

Take a few moments today and intentionally look for occasions to be kind. You can do so at work, in traffic, or when you're walking down the street. As the Dalai Lama once said, "Be kind whenever possible. It is always possible." The chances are endless.

Authenticity

An authentic heart is genuine and acts from truth.

Nobody likes a phony. When you offer a kind act, the recipient will almost always know if you're being genuine or not. If your intent is to be liked, or you're a chronic approval seeker, your actions will most certainly come across as insincere and be rejected. Kindness should never be forced or seem like extra effort. If it doesn't come naturally, this can actually backfire and cause the other person to feel uncomfortable. To be authentic, on the other hand, is to connect with your true essence. This is a vital step toward delivering kindness—you must first instill trust and confidence in the recipient. When people have faith in you, they make a shift from resistance to acceptance. And when you're genuine and give off the energy of being reliable, you won't just find that your acts of kindness are being welcomed, you'll also attract new friends and wonderful opportunities.

The greatest advice I've ever received was from my 80-year-old best friend. Not to be confused with the grandfather I mentioned in Chapter 1, my mother's father was an amazing man who was affectionately known as Moppy. Always full of wit, wisdom, and endless humor, he was such an inspiration to me.

One day while working out of town and struggling emotionally, I called him for some much-needed counsel. As I waited on the other end of the line, expecting some profound wisdom of the ages to flow from his decades of accumulated knowledge, he simply said to me, "Mike, just be yourself."

At first I thought, *Geez, Gramp. Thanks a lot. I'd never even considered that.* But after really considering his advice, it blew me away. He was so right! I'd been so busy trying to escape my past and everything I disliked about myself that I was trying to be somebody I wasn't—no wonder I couldn't "find myself." It was such simple yet profound guidance during that time in my life.

Charity

*A charitable heart gives yet
expects nothing in return.*

Unlike simply being nice, kindness has no attachments, has no conditions, and is completely selfless. Whenever we expect to receive something back from a benevolent gesture, this shows us that the effort wasn't from the heart. It was only our ego's attempt to gain some form of recognition. We'd be wise to avoid even the slightest desire for a thank-you or praise, since kindness is its own reward and should be left at that. If we have expectations and fantasies about an individual's reaction, more times than not we're setting ourselves up for disappointment.

At one point, I would anticipate a gush of love and commendation whenever I did something for another person. What a mistake. I went on like this for quite some time before I finally realized the truth about unconditional giving: it's not about me! I came to understand that kindness meant doing what's best for the person before me, detaching from the outcome, and removing myself from the equation.

Compassion

*A compassionate heart is sensitive
toward all living things.*

When we sincerely empathize, we often see suffering through the eyes of another person (or any living being). This is the state when our heart breaks but then opens as we're moved by love and inspired to take action. The Buddha taught us: "Compassion is that which makes the heart of the good move at the pain of others." The Golden Rule in the Bible tells us: "Do to others as you would have them do to you." And as Mother Teresa so beautifully put it, "The poor do not need our sympathy and our pity. The poor need our love and compassion."

In a world so full of oppression and suffering, we have countless opportunities to show compassion each day. It can be delivered by preparing a warm meal for a homeless person, or we may simply be willing to send out loving energy in the form of a prayer or a silent blessing. The beauty of compassion is that we don't need special skills or qualifications to help others; all we need is our unconditionally loving heart.

Courage

*A courageous heart acts from
love rather than fear.*

Kindness takes tremendous courage. It can vary from smiling at a stranger and saying "Hello" to, in extreme cases, being called upon to swoop in and save the day like a superhero. The key to courageous living begins by acting from our heart and getting out of our analytical mind, where fearful thoughts reside.

A perfect example of a courageous heart was recently broadcast on the evening news. This touching account was about a gentleman at the beach who was unexpectedly called into action when his dog became the target of a rogue shark. Seeing his beloved pet in the mouth of this five-foot puppy-eating machine, the man, with no regard for his own safety, dove headfirst into the ocean to fend off his best friend's attacker! After winning the battle and making it back to dry land with his pooch, he was asked why he'd do something so crazy. His answer was simple and needed no further explanation: "Because I love him, and I thought he deserved whatever I could do."

This story illustrates what it means to act from love rather than fear. If a man can battle a shark to save the life of his pet, perhaps we could, at the very least, find the courage to smile and give some spare change to a stranger on the street—or perform any act of kindness, for that matter.

Enthusiasm

An enthusiastic heart displays limitless energy and passion. For an act of kindness to be effective (and believable), we need to have enthusiasm. Slow, lethargic tonality and weak body language clearly send the message that we're really not into the act . . . but we'll help anyway. This, of course, isn't authentic kindness and simply comes across as obligation or, even worse, helping out of a sense of guilt. When we're enthusiastic, however, we're showing people that we *really* care about them and genuinely *want* to offer assistance. Bringing this passion into any situation sparks excitement and is extremely contagious.

Your enthusiastic heart can quickly shift a person who's feeling discouraged into a new mind-set of optimism and hope. Or, as my inspiring friend John has so beautifully stated: "Just treat people as if it were their birthday—every single day!" Whenever I'm with John, I witness this energizing philosophy in action. He's constantly treating those he interacts with as if it's their special day.

Gratitude

*A grateful heart is content
and filled with appreciation.*

A grateful life is a generous one, and there are two purposes to this seventh element. The first is that a grateful heart serves us personally, because a life that's filled with gratitude is one that's filled with contentment and happiness. People with grateful hearts are always focusing on their blessings, seeing the abundance in their lives, and knowing that they can always share with others because they have so much. These are the individuals who give thanks for even the smallest things and rarely find anything to complain about.

The second part of living gratefully is letting others know just how much we appreciate them and that they are important in our lives. Too often we take people for granted and forget to say "Thank you" or let them know how enriched our lives are because of them.

Obviously, we need to give this gift to family members and friends, but we should also consider showing gratitude to everyone we interact with—including cabdrivers, garbage collectors, and the teachers who work so diligently to give our children the best education possible. Perhaps one of the most important acts of kindness that we can extend to these people is a sincere expression of how thankful we are for what they do. This offering not only energizes and gives the recipient a deep feeling of purpose, it also causes our own hearts to swell in gratitude.

Inspiration

An inspirational heart encourages
and motivates others.

As with the last element, there are also two aspects of an inspirational heart. The first is the ripple effect that your caring nature will have on those around you. As you begin to perform acts of kindness on a regular basis, you'll notice that, in addition to bringing hope to the world and creating your own personal happiness, you're also inspiring others to "pass it on." As I mentioned earlier, kindness is extremely contagious and triggers more of the same type of energy. The individual you're being kind to, and even the observer of an altruistic act, will find him- or herself motivated to go out and do something for someone else. This can inspire one kindhearted deed after another, causing a ripple effect and changing numerous lives.

The other feature of an inspirational heart is that it encourages people when they need a boost in confidence or the assurance that everything will be okay. Cheering on a child stepping onto a baseball field for the very first time, or, in more critical situations, supporting a friend who has been given upsetting news about his or her health, can be a powerful act of kindness. There are times in life when we all need inspiring words or a shoulder to lean on.

Be that source of strength for others, and then when life hands you a challenge, you'll no doubt find someone there for you as well.

Patience

*A patient heart waits and responds
at the proper moment.*

The ninth and final element of a kind heart is a patient heart, which represents an undeniably difficult practice. In our fast-paced, multitasking culture we've been conditioned to believe that patience equals lost time—and, after all, time is money. As a result, we think that losing time means we're losing money, thus losing our edge in life. So, to stay on top, we drive fast, eat fast, work fast, and even play fast. And if our Internet connection doesn't allow us to open a website in 3.2 seconds—we're gone!

The problem with this warp-speed way of life is that we typically end up behaving in rude and ill-mannered ways, disregarding the needs of others. If we could take a deep breath and slow down for a moment, we'd see that opportunities to be kind are all around us. Sometimes it's as simple as listening —*really listening*—to a friend; other times it can be keeping our cool with those who are pushing our buttons. Throughout each day, we're offered dozens of opportunities to practice this much-needed quality in our world. Patience equals peace.

The Tenth Element

In addition to the original 9 elements discussed in this chapter, my experience has led me to add a tenth—what I sometimes refer to as a "secret" element, or a person's own special gift. It's something that both personalizes and completes your kind heart, and it also makes each act of kindness that you perform totally unique.

For example, my own tenth element would be *humor*. I've found that one of the quickest ways to break the ice when attempting a spontaneous act of kindness (especially for strangers) is to make them laugh. If it's appropriate and timed well, a joke or humorous comment can be the perfect way to create an authentic connection or, in many cases, make a new friend.

So what is *your* secret element? Take a moment and really think about that one magical quality you possess that's a gift to the world. Everybody has at least one. It may be a trait or even a talent. Perhaps it's creativity, which is a powerful attribute when it comes to giving to others—after all, sometimes *how* you give is just as important as *what* you give. Maybe it's your ability to share unconditionally with those around you. Whether you contribute material items or your wisdom, this can be a wonderful offering from the heart.

Take a few moments to reflect on your tenth element and write down your responses to the following statements either here or in your notebook or journal. This special gift can be a one-word characteristic or a detailed description of a special talent that blesses the lives of others.

My tenth element is:

_____

_____

It makes the world a better place by:

_____

_____

_____

_____

One example of recently using this element is:

_____

_____

_____

_____

• • •

To apply these tools for kinder living, you simply need to refer back to the power of using the *am I being kind* mantra. By replacing the word *kind* with any of the 9 elements at the appropriate time, you can generate even more inner strength and a much kinder heart. For example, if you're feeling afraid or lacking confidence when you want to help someone, take a deep breath and ask yourself, "Am I being courageous?" Or perhaps you're about to offer a compliment that doesn't feel sincere, in which case you could consider, "Am I being authentic?" After this inner inquiry is made, you can follow up by wondering, "How may I be [patient, courageous, authentic, and so on]?" By consistently applying this formula to everything you do, you'll be speaking the world's most powerful language—the language of love.

The To-Be List

Most people utilize a to-do list in order to get things done each day. Some of us put these daily tasks on paper, while others have the ability to "tattoo" them on their brains. I've found these lists to be the ideal way to keep me on track, while giving me a sense of accomplishment when I can cross out items that are completed throughout the day. But before I begin chipping away at my infinite number of chores, there's another list I create that's imperative to achieving my goals with ease. I call this my *to-be* list.

Creating a to-be list is the ultimate way to prepare yourself for going about your day. When *being* comes before doing, each activity will feel lighter and give you a sense of peace and enjoyment. For example, when I need to return a large number of phone calls, I add *attentiveness* to my to-be list. By focusing on being attentive, I know that my conversations will be much more authentic and enjoyable. Another trait that I often add to my to-be list is *patience*. I find that being patient is vital when attending meetings, running errands, or learning something new. (My wife has this one on her to-be list each day just to live with me.)

I've found that the 9 Elements of a Kind Heart typically dominate my to-be list. Each one fits perfectly with each of my daily actions and the way I communicate. There are, of course, many more ways of being that you could add to your own version. The more personal they are to you, the better they'll work. I've included a typical list that you may see on my desk. I encourage you to create yours and rediscover the truth of your human nature: *that you're a human being, not a human doing.*

To-Do List	To-Be List
Return phone calls	*Attentive*
Tell an associate why we can no longer work together	*Authentic*
Drop off used clothes at the shelter	*Charitable*
Visit my friend who's in the hospital	*Compassionate*
Prepare for an upcoming speech	*Courageous*
Morning and afternoon meetings	*Enthusiastic*
Mail a thank-you note to my wonderful editor	*Grateful*
E-mail my friend who's struggling	*Inspiration*
Renew my driver's license at the DMV	*Patient*
Do *everything* today by *being*	*Loving & Kind*

Now that you understand how to apply the 9 Elements of a Kind Heart, you have all the tools you'll ever need to achieve the fifth and final key described in the previous chapter: *performing acts of kindness.* So if you want to experience the ultimate high in life, don't wait for opportunities—instead, create them now!

Surprising family members or friends with spon-taneous acts of kindness is wonderful and highly encouraged, but performing them for those you don't know is perhaps the greatest way to form a new relationship with a so-called stranger. Is it scary? Sometimes. But I promise you that if you fully engage in the qualities of these loving actions, your life will become more exciting, inspiring, and adventurous every single day!

• • •

In this chapter, you've read about the 9 Elements of a Kind Heart and their characteristics. You've also been introduced to the to-be list and seen how it can support you in applying the 9 elements to your daily life. Chapter 14 provides two true stories that illus-trate all 9 Elements of a Kind Heart in action—plus a secret tenth.

• • • • • •

The 9 Elements of a Kind Heart in Action

This chapter consists of two inspirational stories that exemplify all 9 Elements of a Kind Heart. The first account is one that occurred while I was working with some young adults, and the second one happened during one of my 24 Hours of Kindness events.

A Night on the Town

When I was first asked to spend an evening with a group of "troubled teens," the idea didn't exactly appeal to me. This particular night, however, turned out to be one that I'll never forget. Meeting in the basement of an old church, this collection of reluctant students made it clear that they were *not* there by choice. Their glares and intimidating swaggers had me on edge from the moment I walked through the door . . . especially since one of the adults facilitating the event pointed at a young man and said to me, "If that kid even *looks* at you funny, call the cops immediately!" *Uh . . . okay,* I nervously thought. *What in the world have I gotten myself into?*

The goal seemed simple: I'd explain each of the 9 Elements of a Kind Heart; send the students on a mission of intentional, random acts of kindness; and, after one hour, we'd all return to share our experiences with the group. The downtown area, which was located just a few blocks from the church, would offer numerous chances to make people smile.

After speaking for about 30 minutes, I could see that my enthusiasm and self-effacing humor were actually beginning to win over my audience. Slouching bodies were now sitting upright, and texting teens became intrigued by my promises of euphoric feelings that would accompany a kind deed. Recognizing this small window of opportunity, I knew it was best to cut the educational piece short and get these kids out on the streets as soon as possible.

After I quickly wrapped up my presentation, I made the rules of the activity very clear. Each good-will warrior was given a card with an assignment printed on it. A variety of missions such as "Be kind to the earth—pick up litter," "Smile and say hello to at least ten people," "Return shopping carts to the grocery store," and "Pass out flowers to people you meet" were randomly pulled from a large basket. There were over 50 acts to choose from; however, one of them seemed to be everyone's preferred choice of the night: the opportunity to hand out the canary-yellow, smiley-face balloons hovering in the corner of the otherwise muted room. Other than a few half-hearted teens with an "I'm too cool for this" attitude, it seemed as if everyone wanted to spread helium cheer that evening. As a result, each of us grabbed a few balloons to hand out in addition to performing our selected assignment.

It was a perfect night to be outdoors. It was springtime, which truly is a time of revival in New England. After months of hibernation and ice-cold weather, anything above 50 degrees feels like a tropical paradise to us. And after watching the downtown bank thermometer spike past 60 that day, there was definitely a spirit of renewal in the air. Now just past the dinner hour, the sidewalks were buzzing with shoppers, people walking their dogs, and animated kids riding their bikes. The radiant expression of each person said it all: "Yes! I survived another long winter." This optimistic energy also played in our favor, as those who were out and about seemed, perhaps, happier than normal and more willing to accept our gestures of the heart. Whether it was a smile, a bundle of carnations, or simply having the door held open as they filtered in and out of the convenience store, folks were grateful for our offerings.

After buying ice-cream cones for a couple of kids at the Dairy Queen, my young protégés and I began walking back toward the church. Signs of our mission were now everywhere. Around each corner we'd see a yellow balloon attached to a baby stroller, a child's wrist, or a bicycle weaving through the traffic on Main Street. Women carrying flowers also made it clear that our kindness crew had been in the neighborhood. At this point, we were all excited to share our experiences from the past hour, and couldn't wait to join the rest of the group.

Once we'd all reassembled, we quickly created a circle of chairs. The lethargic energy I'd witnessed as I'd begun my presentation had now been replaced with enthusiasm and a spirit of oneness. The look on each adult's face was of pure shock and amazement.

"This is incredible," one woman said to me. "I've *never* seen them act like this before!"

"Yeah, "I replied, somewhat nonchalantly. "Pretty cool, huh?"

One by one, we shared our tales of encounters with total strangers. Some stories had us laughing like hyenas, while other accounts moved us to tears. There were even a few synchronistic events that had taken place that made us feel as if there was something much larger at play. Whether it was one of our kids who had reunited with a long-lost relative, or that somebody met a person who *really* needed an act of love, the evening definitely proved to be a magical one.

However, one story told by a girl named Alison topped them all. Like most of the group members, Alison hadn't been all that crazy about this event when she'd first arrived. The possibility of being seen "acting all nice and stuff" hadn't sat very well with her. Plus, if other kids heard about this, it would surely tarnish her tough-girl image. It wasn't easy, but with a little coaxing—and the reassurance that this was actually a cool thing to do—she finally agreed to give it a try. With that, Alison was given a fistful of balloons and set free. Just one hour later, a *very* different young lady returned with an experience that touched us to the core . . . and her attitude had changed so drastically that she was courageous enough to share the adventure with us.

Alison's Story

"At first I didn't want to talk to anybody," she began. "I just wanted to hand stuff out." Seeming unsure whether to admit it or not, Alison continued to talk about her encounter without actually telling everyone how much fun she'd had. According to some input from the other kids, though, while she was initially hesitant and aloof, with each kind gesture, Alison's uncertainty and nervous energy were replaced by confidence and joy.

Eventually, and with a twinkle in her eye, she let out the words that we already knew were buried deep inside her: "Yeah, it felt really good." Now grinning, she went on, "I also liked how people looked at me when I gave them something." It was obvious that this night had a profound impact on her. As she continued, what had melted away her tough exterior became clear: the transformational power of gratitude.

With each balloon that Alison handed out, the recipients' appreciation became like shots of adrenaline to her heart. The energy of gratitude was obviously something she hadn't felt in quite some time. But there was much more to this story, and it went far beyond simple acts of kindness and a stranger's thank-you. As we discovered, the final minutes of her journey proved to be a significant test of courage, character, and redemption.

After spending most of the hour cruising the downtown sidewalk, Alison decided to walk over to the local grocery store. With just a single balloon remaining, she only needed to meet and greet one more person. Handing out this final gesture of kindness meant that she could finally return to home base and proclaim, "Mission complete!" Scanning the parking lot and seeing no signs of life, she quickly decided that the store entrance would offer a better opportunity of running into someone.

When Alison first noticed a small body leaning against the brick wall, her initial response was to hurry over there before the individual could leave. She was well aware that everyone was due back at the church soon, and the adults were dead serious about the 7:30 P.M. curfew. Once she could finally make out her target, her swift pace immediately came to a screeching halt. Frozen by what she saw, her shoes now seemed like cement blocks, and both legs became weak.

Alison couldn't believe her eyes—she knew the person who was leaning against the graffiti-covered wall. But perhaps more than just knowing who it was and that her name was Kelley, what she *really* recognized were this girl's eyes . . . and an all-too familiar look of fear. Through teasing, name-calling, and years of intimidation, Alison had once been Kelley's biggest bully. Cowering defensively, this frightened soul continued to look back at her former oppressor with horror. It had been a while since the last cruel incident, but the wounds had obviously never healed. Alison now had to make a difficult decision: continue moving forward or turn and walk away.

With just 20 feet between them, and both girls' hearts pounding like war drums, they both knew there was no backing out. The eye contact had lasted too long, and somebody had to say *something*. But would the words be kind . . . or unkind? Would Kelley run away or stand her ground this time? The truth is, none of us could have guessed what happened next. And while it probably sounds absurd to state this (especially considering the theme of the night), Alison did the very last thing we all expected.

Now standing face-to-face with her once sworn enemy, Alison slowly extended her hand and gently offered the balloon. "Here, Kelley," she said. "This is for you." With her back still pressed against the wall, Kelley looked dazed and confused. She couldn't believe what she'd just heard. Allowing a few seconds to pass, Alison continued: "No, really. Please take it." There was silence, and a few people who were now walking through the parking lot even began to stare.

Finally, Alison completed her mission of the heart with words that no one in that church basement will ever forget: "Kelley, I just want to tell you something. . . . I want you to know how sorry I am for everything that I ever did to you . . . and . . . I hope you will forgive me."

With obvious trepidation, but now sensing that Alison's words were sincere, Kelley reached out and accepted the balloon string. Wrapping it around her finger and looking back with watery eyes, she quietly replied, "Thanks, Alison . . . it's okay . . . I forgive you."

• • •

This story not only teaches us the power of humility and forgiveness, but it also demonstrates the power of all 9 Elements of a Kind Heart. Consider how Alison used each one:

1. *Attentiveness:* She recognized the opportunity to make peace with Kelley.

2. *Authenticity:* She was genuine and acted from her true, loving nature.

3. *Charity:* The balloon and the kind words were given without expecting anything in return.

4. *Compassion:* Her heart opened up to Kelley's suffering.

5. *Courage:* She acted from a place of love rather than fear.

6. *Enthusiasm:* She demonstrated the passionate energy that was necessary to follow through with her commitment.

7. *Gratitude:* She was grateful that Kelley accepted her apology.

8. *Inspiration:* This story now inspires thousands of people.

9. *Patience:* Even though Alison was in a hurry to return to the church, she took the time to reach out to Kelley.

10. *Secret Element: Humility:* She dropped her guard, allowed herself to be vulnerable, and even admitted that she was wrong.

9 Elements at 7-Eleven

With just five hours remaining of the second annual 24 Hours of Kindness event, I knew that extra caution was a must this time of the night. After all, the city streets were home to many *interesting* people.

It was just after 2 A.M., and my goal at this point was to find anyone who needed hot coffee or something to eat. The rain was coming down pretty hard, so I figured that underneath a bridge or railroad pass would be a good place to look.

I'd spent an hour with one homeless man earlier that evening who'd shown me once again that spiritual teachers are everywhere, and I was still overwhelmed by the advice he'd given me. The few dollars I'd placed in his hand weren't adequate payment for the lessons he'd placed in my heart. His wisdom would ultimately inspire thousands as I conveyed his message during my presentations in the months that followed.

Driving slowly while scanning the desolate streets, I decided to pass the all-night convenience store one more time even though I'd been there just hours before and had offered help to a handful of strangers. But as I entered the parking lot again, everything seemed *very* different, especially the clientele standing outside in a cloud of cigarette smoke. Finding my courageous heart, I slowly pulled into a space off to the side.

Through the smoky rain, I immediately noticed a woman sitting under the green-and-orange awning. Not only did she appear cold and wet, she also seemed to be in distress. With her head nestled tightly between her knees, the subtle bounce of her body told me that she was probably crying.

Now out of my car, I began to make my way through the parking lot. Hearing the strange pattern of my footsteps, her head quickly popped up, and her watery eyes seemed to say, "Thank God you're here. I've been waiting for you." But seeing my unfamiliar face, her head dropped again, as if to say, "Oh . . . I thought you were someone else."

As I got closer, I could see that she was wrapped in a thin layer of clothing with only a waterlogged jacket to protect her. I also noticed that strands of yellow hair were stuck to her face as a result of the rain and her tears. Trying not to frighten her, I asked with a tone of concern, "Are you okay?"

Slowly, she raised her head, only this time with a look of confusion. In a weak voice she answered, "Oh, yeah . . . I'm fine . . . thank you." Her eyes told a different story, though.

"Would you like a blanket?" I continued.

Her face instantly softened. "That would be nice," she whispered back.

"How about something hot to drink, too," I added. This time the woman shyly looked away, almost seeming embarrassed. I quickly followed up with another question: "Are you hungry?"

Finally, she responded with what seemed like a touch of insecurity, "Could I please have a cappuccino?" The way she asked was so sweet.

Smiling back at her, I replied, "Of course you can," hoping that there actually was a cappuccino machine in the store.

As I turned toward the door, a man who seemed to be half my height barked directly at me, "Hey, I know what she likes. Let me help you!"

Looking down, I noticed that his hair and scraggly beard were nearly as long as his entire body. I tried not to make assumptions, but his olive-colored jacket and backpack made me think, *Homeless war vet.* This unfair assessment was likely due to my infatuation with Chuck Norris Vietnam War movies from back in the '80s. "Sure," I answered. "Come inside, and I'll buy one for you, too."

Hearing this, another man with long, flowing hair looked toward me as if to say, "Hey, what about me?"

Beside him, yet another guy, this one with a shopping cart, also began to stare. Sensing their need for caffeine, I asked, "Would you guys like something, too?"

After filling half a dozen cups with java, I carefully brought the tray to the counter. Sifting through my pockets, I began looking for the kindness cash that I used for situations such as this. As I finally located a crumpled ten-dollar bill, the cashier, who had been watching me, smiled and said, "Hey man, what's up?"

"Just buying coffee for some friends," I replied.

Seeing my intention (and obviously knowing the crowd I was about to serve), she insisted, "Nah, it's on me tonight."

I was shocked. "What do you mean?" I shouted back with gusto.

Still grinning warmly, she explained, "I mean take it. No charge. I think it's nice what you're doing out there." Her kind offer had blown me away. I'd been gifting food and coffee to strangers all day, but only now did I understand what people actually felt when they received kindness. *So cool,* I thought.

For the next three hours I sat in the rain listening to incredible stories of resilience and heartbreak. The woman who had originally drawn me into the parking lot shared how she had recently lost her children and her home, and her father had committed suicide. She'd tried to make it to the shelter that night, but the door was locked when she arrived.

My long-haired, vertically challenged friend Lefty also shared his tale, which included 50-plus years on the streets. "You just get used to it," he said with a nonchalant tone.

Next was Brad. A bearded fellow with dirty blond hair, he'd recently been jumped by a group of rabid teens who stole his bags and what little cash he'd had.

Seeing my expression of disgust, everyone piped up with comments like, "Oh, it happens all the time around here. That's why we try not to walk alone."

Then there was The Can Man. Still seething with anger from something that had happened earlier, he continued complaining about a "thief" in his territory. As he leaned on a cart filled with plastic and aluminum containers, he made it perfectly clear that stealing from *his* trash cans and Dumpsters meant war.

And finally, a young entrepreneur in her 20s told stories of paying her rent through prostitution and other creative means. "But that was a long time ago," she said. "Now I got a job."

As the night wore on, a steady stream of people filtered in and out of our circle. Some were looking for companionship, while others just needed to "bum a smoke." But as I continued listening, buying additional rounds of coffee, and learning about life on the street, I couldn't help but feel a strange sense of belonging. Although I was a stranger to everyone in this little community, each person welcomed me with open arms. It truly was like a family. Time and again I witnessed kindness in action, but rather than kindness extended *by* me, it was offered *to* me. These misunderstood souls shared what little they had, kept no secrets, never judged, and simply accepted me (and each other) unconditionally. Isn't that what a *real* family is supposed to do, after all?

Three profound hours later (and enough second-hand smoke to last me a lifetime), it was time for me to say good-bye. I wanted to make a few more stops before wrapping up the 24 Hours of Kindness. Feeling somewhat off-balance, I could tell that fatigue was now setting in as I stumbled toward my car. Opening the hatchback, I peeled off the clammy sweatshirt I'd worn all night and began looking for something dry to wear. Lefty, noticing the vibrant array of carnations in my backseat, became curious (which actually would have been a more fitting name for him) and barked at me, "Hey, what are all those flowers for?"

He was now peeking in my windows like a kid at a candy store as I explained my 24-hour mission to him. "I've been handing out carnations since 7 A.M. yesterday morning, simply to brighten people's day."

"Man, you must be tired," he said.

"Yeah, just a little," I replied.

Now only halfheartedly listening to me, Lefty finally revealed what was actually on his mind: "Can I have some of these?"

Curious about what he could possibly do with flowers at 5:30 in the morning, I smiled and jokingly asked, "Lefty, do you have a date this morning?"

"Very funny," he growled back. "No . . . I just thought we should do something for *her*." He turned his head toward the store, and I could see that he was referring to the clerk behind the ten-foot sheet of glass.

Lefty was so right; if anyone here deserved an act of kindness, it was definitely this cashier. Not only had she given away free coffee and shared the employees-only restroom, she'd also ignored the store's no-loitering policy the entire night. Pulling the two buckets forward, I said, "That's an awesome idea. Take as many as you'd like, my friend."

One by one, he carefully made his selection while hundreds of carnations reflected in his twinkling eyes. "These are really nice!" he yelped.

Moments later, I watched his tiny body hobble through the door. Finally making his way to the front of the line, he offered the woman two dozen pink-and-white expressions of gratitude. The look on her face made my heart completely skip a beat. In addition to her joyful response, I noticed that Lefty's four-and-a-half-foot frame now seemed as if it were eight feet tall.

Right at this moment, I realized that changing the world truly does begin this way. By simply acknowledging each other with sincere love and gratitude, we all become a part of the collective family of human kindness.

• • •

Consider how the 9 Elements of a Kind Heart were used in this story:

1. *Attentiveness:* I noticed the woman in distress and recognized the needs of others throughout the night.

2. *Authenticity:* I interacted with these people because I truly *wanted* to be with them, not out of obligation or guilt.

3. *Charity:* Coffee, food, conversation, and advice were all given away that night without anyone expecting a thing in return.

4. *Compassion:* We all learned a little bit about the others who were there and displayed sincere empathy and compassion for their suffering.

5. *Courage:* It took courage for me to pull into a dark parking lot at 2 A.M. and approach complete strangers!

6. *Enthusiasm:* Maintaining positive energy during the entire night told everyone that I truly cared and wanted to be there.

7. *Gratitude:* Each offering I made was accepted with sincere gratitude. And *I* was grateful for the way they accepted me into their circle.

8. *Inspiration:* The clerk, inspired by my kindness, offered free coffee to all. Lefty, inspired by my mission, also decided to pass it on to her.

9. *Patience:* As you can imagine, spending three hours in the rain, inhaling second-hand smoke, and listening to dozens of stories . . . required a great deal of patience.

10. *Secret Element: Curiosity:* Instead of judging the people I met in the parking lot, I was

curious about them. Curiosity is the heart's way of curing a judgmental mind.

• • •

You've now seen the 9 Elements of a Kind Heart applied in two real-life situations. In the next chapter, you'll discover ways to recognize and create opportunities for kindness and learn the benefits of living a heart-centered life.

You'll also finally be making your commitment to *living a life of kindness* as you sign the final contract with yourself.

• • • • • •

Chapter 15

Making the Choice: Kindness as *Your* Way of Life

I have found that there are three primary ways in which we can offer kindness to the world. They include giving *personally, materially,* and *spiritually.* As you might imagine, each one can be performed by itself, or can be combined to create even greater power. I've described them next, followed by a few suggestions for putting them into action.

Giving Personally

Personal acts of kindness can be offered in the form of a warm smile, a hug, a compliment, listening, letting someone go ahead of you in traffic, helping a neighbor with yard work, or anything that doesn't require money or a physical item. Have some fun with it! Use your imagination and creativity to invent new personal acts of kindness that suit your situation. The opportunities to brighten someone's day are endless.

9 Examples of Giving Personally

1. Give up your seat to someone on the bus, train, or subway.

2. Shovel snow or mow the lawn for a friend or neighbor.

3. Let someone who has fewer groceries go ahead of you in line.

4. If someone looks lost, offer directions or show them the way.

5. Be kind to the earth by picking up litter.

6. When you see people posing for a group photo, offer to take the picture so everyone can be in it.

7. Look someone in the eye when you say thank you . . . and really mean it.

8. Give someone the gift of your smile.

9. Talk less and listen more . . . *really* listen.

Giving Materially

Material contributions include financial gifts or physical items. Donations to a charity or church, buying a co-worker lunch, giving away unused items such as clothing and old furniture, or surprising a stranger with a free sundae at an ice-cream shop are all examples of material offerings.

9 Examples of Giving Materially

1. Send a note or card to a few friends to let them know how important they are to you.

2. Buy a homeless person a meal or a cup of coffee.

3. Offer someone your umbrella when it's raining.

4. Donate clothes and other items to a local shelter.

5. When you're finished reading your newspaper or magazine in a public place, offer it to another person.

6. Put change in someone's parking meter to pay for his or her space.

7. Purchase a bouquet of flowers, drop them off at a hospital, and ask to have them delivered to a patient who doesn't receive many visitors.

8. Deliver freshly baked cookies to city workers.

9. Tape four quarters to a vending machine along with a note that reads: "This is a random act of kindness just for you."

Giving Spiritually

Perhaps the most powerful gift we can offer comes in the form of prayer, silent blessings, or positive energy sent to those in need. Meditating on peace or transmitting loving thoughts out into the world each day has the power to transform lives . . . and heal our planet.

9 Examples of Giving Spiritually

1. Meditate each day on world peace.

2. Pray for a friend who's struggling financially.

3. While sitting in traffic, send out silent blessings to those around you.

4. When a discouraging story is reported on the news, pray for all those involved.

5. Think kind thoughts about yourself.

6. Think kind thoughts about individuals you don't get along with.

7. Send out positive energy to people who seem unhappy.

8. Say a prayer of thanks for all of the blessings in your life.

9. Want more for others than you do for yourself.

A Road Map to the Heart

In June of 2008, The Kindness Center embarked on its most epic journey to date: The 3,000 Miles of Kindness. During this cross-country voyage, we drove from Los Angeles to Maine, reaching out to as many people as possible. At each stop we capitalized on numerous opportunities to help people, such as changing a flat tire; buying meals for people at truck stops and all-night diners; cleaning up litter on streets and beaches; purchasing coffee and breakfast for people each morning; handing out flowers and pastries in Brooklyn, New York; and much more.

Throughout the trip, I learned that time and sincere listening are among the greatest gifts we can offer one another. I would start each day by getting up early to seek out other road warriors, offering them breakfast in the hopes that they'd share their cross-country adventures with me. I always love hearing the stories related by fellow travelers. Driving through 18 states and covering 3,570.6 miles (to be exact), I met dozens of people across the U.S., but it was one morning in Arizona when I learned just how important it is to open our hearts to everyone we meet.

Figuring that the motel lobby would be a good place to make new friends, I walked in at 6 A.M. to find a handful of early birds searching for some much-needed caffeine. After exchanging a few friendly words with the housekeeping staff, I noticed a man peacefully standing in the corner sipping his coffee while watching strangers snatch up free maps from a rack before they checked out. His salt-and-pepper beard and curly gray hair made me guess that he was somewhere in his late 40s to mid-50s. He seemed quite content, but his posture revealed a hint of both sadness and concern—he also appeared to be traveling alone. I have no idea why, but there was something intriguing about his presence, and I felt a strong urge to learn more about him. Summoning my courageous heart, I made my move and offered a customary "How are ya this morning?"—hoping he would be up for a little road talk or light conversation.

His name was Ted, and he was indeed traveling alone. His journey had begun in the Deep South, and he was making his way to California to visit his children—a teenage son and a daughter in her early 20s. His goal was to put in another full day of driving and arrive at his destination before sundown so he wouldn't miss his daughter's birthday. I got the impression that it had been quite some time since he'd seen either of them.

We got into a casual discussion, talking about life on the road, outrageous gas prices, and his favorite stops thus far. As time passed, I started noticing a softness in his eyes that was saying, "Hey, can I talk to you? . . . No, I mean *really* talk to you." My own eyes must have said, "Yes, I'm here for you," because seconds later the floodgates were thrown wide open.

What had only moments before seemed like a simple story of a man visiting his children quickly turned into an emotional exchange between two kindred souls—and it was a conversation I'll never forget.

The heartbreaking truth was that Ted had a brain tumor and was taking what would likely be his last journey across the country. It was also his final attempt to heal the broken relationship that he had with his daughter. Hearing this news, I uncharacteristically found myself at a loss for words. Overwhelmed by the enormity of his situation, I felt completely powerless. As time went on, I realized that I didn't need to say anything at all; the greatest gift I could give Ted at that moment was an attentive mind and heart.

For the next hour, we shared our philosophies on life and its true meaning. We also created strategies for making peace with his daughter. It was such a tender dialogue, filled with an equal exchange of affection and friendship. When it was finally time to say good-bye and go our separate ways, my once broken heart was now overflowing and completely restored. Our conversation allowed me to see the perfection of the universe and understand that we don't always have to fix everything in life. Sometimes our only job is to simply listen with love.

The Ripple Effect

I'll never forget my first public talk about The Kindness Center and my vision of creating a kinder world. It had only been a few months since I'd begun spreading my message, so my material was pretty thin. At that point, I hadn't yet developed any solid, teachable philosophies, so I needed to rely on a handful of stories about performing spontaneous acts of kindness.

As I've mentioned, one of my favorite activities is offering to buy coffee for strangers in local shops and cafés. It is simple, affordable, and, especially, safe— the recipient can watch the coffee being made rather than trust something that is handed to them on the street by a potential "nut." Once people understand my intent, each cup I offer is followed by acceptance and elation. I have never been rejected. In addition to face-to-face caffeinated kindness, I also love to utilize the drive-through window. Each week I pay for my coffee in this way and then tell the cashier taking my money: "I'll pay for the car behind me, too." Whenever I do this, I quickly hand over the extra cash and speed off to avoid being thanked or recognized. It is exhilarating for me.

Shortly after telling the audience about my most recent coffee-shop adventures, a woman in the back of the room shot her hand into the air with a look of bewilderment and excitement. Her expression told me that she didn't have a question, but rather wanted to share her thoughts on the current subject. When I called on her, she leaned forward intently and said, "I live in the same town as you, and a guy did that coffee thing for my husband . . . and I now know it was you."

The intensity in her voice made me wonder if I'd done something offensive, or even bought her spouse a bad cup of joe. Trying to keep things light, I smiled and replied, "Was the coffee *reeeeally* bad?"

The crowd erupted with laughter, but the woman maintained her serious tone. Now sensing her intensity, everyone became quiet as she spoke again with passion in her voice. "No, you don't understand. Ever since that day, my husband has been a different person. He now buys coffee for other people, pays the highway tolls for cars behind us, and he's . . . well, if I'm being honest . . . a nicer guy than he's ever been." The room went silent. Seconds later, the stillness turned into a buzz of amazement over the life-changing power of $1.65.

This was the first time I truly started to understand the power of the *ripple effect* and how it can change the world. In the beginning, I'd only focused on how the original recipient was affected and never fully considered the bigger picture of his or her passing it on. As I receive e-mails from around the world, from people sharing one amazing story after another, I now realize that this is how a worldwide shift in consciousness can begin. We may never personally see or understand the impact of one kind act, but rest assured that it doesn't stop with one individual. It's an infinite beam of light that travels around the planet touching one life after another.

The Greek storyteller Aesop once said: "No act of kindness, no matter how small, is ever wasted." This is an important lesson as we consider not only the ripple effect, but also the *snowball effect*. Small acts of kindness that are passed on to others often grow in size and become much larger than the original act itself.

Invisible Acts of Kindness

There is incredible power in the benevolent practice of performing *invisible acts of kindness*. Thoughts and feelings of love toward another person carry with them an undeniable energy that makes an impact on both the giver and the receiver. They're especially effective when we can't find the courage to express ourselves in words and are compelled to share what is in our hearts. We can do this with friends and family members, co-workers, and, of course, complete strangers.

I recommend performing at least three invisible acts of kindness per day. You can do so with someone who appears to be down and having a bad day, or even with those who seem completely at ease. At times, I find myself picking out individuals in traffic and directing thoughts of joy and peace their way. This is a great way to pass the time while stopped at a red light. Call me crazy, but I've witnessed people smile for no apparent reason. It's also a wonderful way to build up your own confidence before performing physical acts of kindness. Begin by projecting loving thoughts toward someone, and soon the words and actions will follow.

The Heart's Perspective

It had been one of those days. My mood had pretty much hit rock bottom, so I decided that I needed to get out of the house for a while. It was early spring, and I thought that the fresh air would do me some good. Fortunately, I've learned by now that the surest way to change my energy is by going out to do something for someone else. So, jumping into my truck, I took a trip to Old Orchard Beach to check out the downtown area. I figured I'd take a walk around and maybe find a person or two whose day could use some brightening.

As I drove down the main drag toward the ocean, I noticed a man curled up in a tight ball outside the Laundromat. Wrapped in an old black trench coat, he seemed cold and appeared to be perhaps homeless. Seeing the bakery just a few doors down, I thought it would be the perfect opportunity to do something for this despondent-looking soul. Surely he would welcome a cup of hot coffee and a snack.

After parking my truck, I headed across the street. As I got closer, I could see that the man was very dirty. His hair was matted down as if it hadn't been washed in weeks, and he seemed even more dejected than my original impression. Sitting on the sidewalk, legs crossed with his head down, this man's only companion was a half-empty pack of cigarettes resting between his feet. My heart was now starting to beat faster and faster as the adrenaline rush that typically accompanies a spontaneous act of kindness was now coursing through my veins.

Now only a few feet away from him, I was ready to make my move. At that point I took a deep breath, smiled, and was about to say "Hello" . . . when I found myself ducking a tattered coat sleeve and a wildly swinging fist!

"Get the hell away from me!" he screamed. *Both* fists were now flailing about as if bees were swarming around his head.

Jumping back, I told him it was okay and that I just wanted to say hi, but there was simply no reasoning with this guy. I was stunned, embarrassed, and, quite honestly, a little offended. I mean, I'd never been rejected like this before, and I'd only wanted to buy him something to eat!

Walking away, and not wanting to upset him any more, I could hear mumbled obscenities directed my way. *Maybe I should have just stayed home,* I thought.

When I got back inside my truck, I sat there for a few minutes trying to figure out what had just happened. I knew in my heart that I shouldn't take this personally, but it still hurt. I also felt bad about upsetting this man. Ultimately, I decided that it was best to just let it go.

As I turned around and headed up the street, I could still see him sitting on the cold sidewalk, watching over his pack of Marlboros. An unexpected new emotion came over me as I slowed down and looked directly at him. I began to have an overwhelming sense of empathy and compassion. My heart was now opening for the guy who had, just minutes before, taken a swing at me. As I passed by, I began to realize that although he could reject me on a physical plane, he simply couldn't stop me from sending him sincere thoughts of love and kindness—which is exactly what I did for the rest of my ride home.

The Benefits of Kindness

The benefits of adopting kindness as a way of life are nothing short of astonishing. Spend a little time reading about this subject and you'll find that people (like you) who practice the 5 Keys to Kindness are much more likely to experience the following:

- Positive personal and professional relationships
- Vibrant health
- Dozens of caring friends
- Confidence and self-appreciation
- A sense of inner peace
- Inspiring careers
- Greater income and more overall abundance
- The respect of others
- Positive reputations
- A deep sense of purpose and belonging
- Lasting marriages
- Longer life expectancy
- Less stress
- Better sleep at night
- Less drama and conflict

- Less anxiety and depression
- Authentic happiness
- Strong spiritual connections

Shifting Your Perspective

Another powerful benefit of kindness is the unde-niable *attractor factor.* In recent years there has been much talk about the Law of Attraction, especially with the tremendous success of books such as *The Secret.* I've found that this philosophy has some pow-erful lessons and ideas worth considering; however, I believe that there's a missing ingredient in some of the products and courses that teach it.

In most of the material I've seen, the primary message has been: "You attract what you think about," with the emphasis on your *feelings* as the pri-mary way to manifest your desires into material form. For instance, if you want to attract a new romance into your life, it's not only important to visualize the qualities that you desire in a person, but you also must generate the intense emotions of what it would *feel like* to have him or her in your life. This sentiment is believed to be the frequency that will pull your ideal mate into your reality. Of course, this technique can also be used for material items or bringing any kind of abundance to fruition.

Personally, I've noticed this principle to be true. On days when I'm in a good mood, or when I'm feeling especially grateful, I tend to attract positive people and circumstances. And when I'm grouchy, more often than not, depressing situations and despondent individuals seem to show up repeatedly throughout my day. This is simply another demonstration that energy attracts like energy.

With that said, I've discovered another truth to this philosophy—and perhaps a much simpler way to view it. Through my own experiences and by observing others, I've come to believe without a doubt that . . . *you attract what you are.* People who are loving, kind, compassionate, and always looking to serve others will attract loving, kind, compassionate people who want to serve them! This is why generous individuals tend to experience so much abundance. It seems as though the more they give, the more that flows into their lives!

By extension, the opposite is also true. Those who are constantly treating others in harsh ways and focusing on their own needs will attract the same types of people and conditions.

This is the very essence of personal magnetics. Simply put, whatever you want to experience in life, *be it.* The universe is a cosmic mirror that will only give back what you project onto it. When you're loving and kind, this mirror (life) will always smile back and love you. Yell, scream, and be rude—and you'll get more of the same.

Looking back at the seven choices we discussed in Part II of this book, you can see how they relate to this lesson of the cosmic mirror. If you're constantly acting like a victim, being resentful, abusing yourself, feeling meaningless and insignificant, getting into unhealthy relationships, and especially, being unkind, life isn't going to love you back. Unfortunately, individuals who consistently struggle have yet to discover this powerful truth . . . but being happy really is that simple. When you make choices from the heart and radiate the qualities of love and kindness, you're likely to find that you'll get the same in return.

Making the Choice

You may have noticed by now that the pathway to creating a better life and a more peaceful world doesn't require a special degree, a particular faith, or even financial wealth—happier lives are our birthrights.

Margaret Mead once said: "Never doubt that a small group of thoughtful, committed citizens can change the world; indeed, it's the only thing that ever has." Each one of us could be likened to a single drop of rain, which when combined with other droplets can turn puddles into streams, streams into rivers, and ultimately, create vast bodies of water.

Your life represents a single drop of kindness that, when pooled with others, will create an ocean of love that reaches every shoreline and being on Earth.

In the next few paragraphs you'll find portrayals of two individuals on very different paths. By looking at the characteristics of each person, making this final choice will perhaps be the easiest yet.

As a person who lives a life of unkindness, I feel: depressed, friendless, disliked, or even hated.

Others see me as: selfish, mean-spirited, angry, hateful, malicious, dishonest, spiteful, egotistical, unfriendly, hostile, ruthless, prejudiced, and judgmental.

I could be described as: a victim, resentful, abusive, uninspired, insignificant, and . . . an energy vampire!

As a person who lives a life of kindness, I feel: respected, loved, spiritual, compassionate, generous, significant, creative, passionate, happy, helpful, vibrant, energized, vigorous, admired, and confident.

I'm also living all 9 Elements of a Kind Heart. My heart is: attentive, authentic, charitable, compassionate, courageous, enthusiastic, grateful, inspirational, and patient.

And I can be described as: responsible, forgiving, healthy, living my dreams, purposeful, and surrounded by positive and loving relationships!

Questions for the Heart

So what kinds of experiences do you want to have? Please take a few moments to reflect on the life you desire: your friends, your well-being, your passions, your connection with the world around you, and the impact you want to make. Then decide if you're willing to choose kindness.

By making this final commitment, you're assuring yourself a lifetime of inner peace and joy. Please sign the following contract with yourself:

I have chosen a life of kindness because I want to experience more _____

_____ *in my life.*

Your signature _____

Date _____

Choices now made: *responsibility, forgiveness, wellness, dreaming big, living a life of purpose, positive relationships,* and *a life of kindness*

The Livingkindness Pledge

This pledge was developed by The Kindness Center and is used in many of the schools we work with. Each class repeats this pledge following the school's morning announcements. Although it was initially designed for students, anyone can use it to create the positive frame of mind needed to begin each day:

> *During this day, I will choose kindness in all that I think, say, and do. I will be kind to myself. I will be kind to others. I will be kind to the earth. By livingkindness each day, I create happiness in my life . . . and in the lives of others.*

• • •

Congratulations! You've now made all seven choices that will undeniably lead you to a happier, healthier, and, of course, kinder life. But this book isn't finished yet! There's still one more—somewhat surprising—piece to the kindness puzzle, and you'll find it in the next chapter.

• • •　• • •

Chapter 16

Receiving Kindness

The topic of *livingkindness* would be incomplete without noting the importance of *receiving* the kind acts others offer us. I discovered this truth one cold January day.

It was one of those bone-chilling afternoons when you just don't want to go outdoors. Subzero temperatures are a part of living in Maine, but personally, I feel the less time spent outside during the middle of winter, the better. As I ran a few errands that day, I strategically planned them based on whether or not the establishments had drive-through service. A quick stop at the post office, the bank, and perhaps the coffee shop were the only things on my list, and they'd all allow me to remain in my truck.

After completing all my tasks within about 30 minutes, I was on my way home. Traveling down the road that runs straight though the heart of town, I could make out a familiar figure standing on the edge of the street. I'd seen this person dozens of times sleeping on sidewalks and benches, but what she was doing at this moment was completely out of character. As I approached her, I could see a tiny thumb protruding from her ragged coat sleeve; to my astonishment, I realized that *she was hitchhiking.*

Claudette is our town's most well-known homeless person. For as long as I can recall, she has been walking the streets carrying around more than a dozen plastic shopping bags. No one really knows what is *in* the bags, and quite honestly, no one wants to. Standing at barely four feet tall, she's a familiar sight from a distance, but not a familiar face. Due to the massive curvature in her spine, Claudette's horseshoe-shaped posture causes her face to be hidden, and it seems as if she's always looking down. It's a heartbreaking and painful sight to see her constantly dragging her belongings down the sidewalk.

When I saw her there, looking as if she were frozen and standing in a sea of plastic bags, I wondered where she could possibly be going. I figured it must have been an important destination, because despite her physical challenges, Claudette walked everywhere. Wrapped from head to toe in multiple layers, it was obvious that she was quite cold. Her misshapen body and drooping head reminded me of a wilted flower that was completely out of its element.

Now just seconds away from passing her by, I realized that I needed to make a decision. My mind began to race. *Do I stop . . . or do I go home?* There was a ferocious battle raging between my head and my heart, but it was actually my foot that would make the final call. It was simply a matter of braking or accelerating. And since this is a book about kindness, you can probably already guess what I did. Right?

Wrong! . . . I drove right by her.

Yes, it is true. My selfish "*It's too cold . . . I just want to drink my coffee . . . I've got lots of work to do*" mindset kicked in, which meant that I left this poor soul standing on an icy street corner. I was so disappointed with myself. *Founder of The Kindness Center—yeah, right,* I thought. But I also knew that fear was the biggest reason I didn't stop. I admit it: I was scared of a four-foot, 90-pound, 70-something-year-old homeless woman.

Now just minutes from my house and feeling like a phony (trust me, it's not always easy being known as The Kindness Guy), I knew that this decision would haunt me all day. But I was also aware that it wasn't too late to make another choice: *the choice to turn around*. Looking down at my hand gripping the steering wheel, I saw the electric blue wristband that reads *"am I being kind"* staring back at me. I could now feel a smile begin to form on my face as I muttered the words: "Damn blue wristband."

· · ·

Seeing my truck pull up to the curb, my frozen little friend displayed a burst of pure energy—she looked genuinely grateful. Before I could even get out of the truck to offer my assistance, she'd already snatched up her bags and had begun hobbling my way.

"Would you like a ride?" I asked.

Still unable to see her face, I knew that I'd have to listen very closely. "Oh, yes. Thank you," her squeaky voice exclaimed. "I just need to get to Walmart."

I was instantly relieved when I heard that her destination was only a ten-minute drive away. "Absolutely," I said, while placing her possessions into the bed of my truck. I tried not to make it obvious, but I preferred that her dozen or so mystery bags remain in the back rather than riding up front with us.

Perhaps what *was* obvious was that within seconds of helping her into the cab, my window was cranked all the way down. Yes, it was absolutely freezing outside . . . but the smell was just too much to bear. Leaning ever so slightly to my left, I kept trying to suck in fresh air as our conversation began.

"My name is Claudette," she said. Now slightly looking my way, I was finally able to get a good look at her face. The lines in her skin seemed more like trenches, and the wiry whiskers protruding from her lip reminded me of a wise old alley cat. It was quite obvious that she hadn't had an easy life.

Turning away from the window, I exhaled and then answered. "Hi Claudette, my name is Michael."

"What a nice name!" she commented with enthusiasm.

The more I looked at her, the more she reminded me of someone I knew. This seemed like a strange thought since I really didn't know anyone with her unique features. Before I could even thank her for complimenting me on my name, she spoke again: "What a nice day out there, eh?"

This seemed like an unusually optimistic outlook for a homeless woman on a 15-degree day. Trying to remain in her spirit of positive energy, I replied, "Yes, the sun is nice and bright today."

Not surprisingly, Claudette had an interesting story. In just ten short minutes she was able to paint a vivid picture of her fascinating life. She spoke of her home in Montreal and her mother, and revealed that she'd been on the streets for a very long time.

As she continued talking about the past, and even her current situation, I noticed that something was missing. While she was sharing her seemingly less-than-ideal journey (and for the second time made reference to the "beautiful day"), I noticed that not once did Claudette do what most of us do as we go through our day: complain. Not once did she say, "Look at what our government and this economy has done to me!" or "Society is cruel and life is unfair." Not once did she play the "blame game" or the victim card. On the contrary, she only mused about sweet memories and the beauty of today. *Mother Teresa!* my mind exclaimed. *Yes, that's who she reminds me of . . . Mother Teresa.*

When we finally arrived at our destination, Claudette asked if I would drop her off somewhere near the front. Figuring this would only take a minute or two, I pulled right up to the curb and parked beside the large automatic doors. "Thank you. This is perfect," she said with gratitude in her voice.

Opening my door, I asked her to wait so I could help her down—just getting her into the truck had been difficult, and I definitely didn't want to see her take a fall as she got out. Holding her by the hand, I gently guided her to the ground. "You're so nice," her soft voice squeaked.

Next were her bags. "Oh, just put them on the bench over there," she suggested. Gathering them up, I carefully placed each one on the wooden bench that was now clearly marked: "This seat is taken." Setting the last bag down, I turned to say good-bye, only to find Claudette back at my truck digging intently through her pockets. From a few feet away, I could see her tiny hand holding four crumpled-up dollar bills.

With the zeal of a Wild West gunslinger, her arm flew from her side as if someone had just yelled, "Draw!" "Here," she demanded. "This is for you." I was completely taken aback. "You take this," she barked. "Gas is expensive, and your time is very valuable." I simply could not believe that this sweet little homeless woman was trying to give *me* money! Putting my hands over my heart, I thanked her for the generous offer but told her that I simply couldn't accept it.

"It's cold today," I said. "I just wanted to help you out."

But she would hear none of it.

For the next several minutes, she continued pushing the four dollars toward my chest. And with every attempt she made, I graciously refused. I felt bad, but there was just *no way* I could take her money. But what made me feel even worse was the fact that I wasn't even looking at her face. Finally, I dropped to a knee so I could see her eyes. I wanted her to know how much I appreciated this kind offer.

At this point, I started to get that "somebody's watching me" feeling, as I now realized people had been stopping to witness the strange event taking place in front of the store. I can only imagine what this bizarre scene must have looked like to those who were walking by. I mean, here I was, on my knees in the Walmart parking lot while a little homeless woman was trying to give me money! The expression of each passerby pretty much said it all: *Wow, that guy must be really bad off!*

There was no doubt about it; she wanted me to have that cash in the worst way. But she could also tell that I was far too stubborn to accept it. Frustrated and completely exhausted, Claudette finally gave up. "All right, then," she said. "You see me around town all the time. If you ever need four dollars, you know where to find it."

Rising to my feet, I gently touched her shoulder and said, "Thank you, Claudette. That's more than fair, but please just pass it on to somebody else for me. Okay?"

Nodding her head in agreement, she thanked me again and slowly began to walk away.

• • •

Normally after performing an act of kindness I'm on an absolute high. The sensation I get from doing something for another person is indescribable. But not today. Within seconds of exiting the parking lot, my heart was as cold as the temperature outside. Even my stomach ached. There was an unfamiliar sensation, an emptiness, that I'd never experienced after helping a stranger.

At first it was all very confusing . . . but then it hit me. I finally understood why I felt so depleted. I realized that I'd just stopped Claudette from doing the very thing I'm trying to inspire the world to do: *be kind.* I'd also deprived her of the joyous feelings that accompany giving, which I so often speak about. The fact is, *without receiving, there can be no giving.* The exchange of these two energies is absolutely vital if we're to create a kinder world. I now see that God had shown up—in the form of a little homeless woman—to teach me this profound lesson.

Whether it's a compliment, a financial gift, help with a project, or even a smile, I now see that receiving kindness from others is actually my gift back to them. And by accepting it with sincere gratitude, both the giver and the recipient ultimately experience the power of a fully functioning heart.

• • •

You've just finished the last formal chapter in *am I being kind*. But before we end our journey together, I'd like to share one final story in the Afterword. Not only is it one of the most treasured experiences of my life, but it will also sum up the entire meaning of this book . . . in two succinct words.

• • • • • •

Afterword

I'll never forget the day my grandfather, Moppy, called me to get my opinion on something rather profound. This was an unfamiliar situation for me, because I was usually the one looking to him for advice. It was during the time when his health was rapidly deteriorating, and there was some uncertainty as to how much longer he'd be with us—his ongoing battle with cancer was a heartbreaking ordeal for our family.

We all loved this man so much and couldn't bear the thought of his passing, and one of our efforts to keep him with us for as long as possible was to help him quit smoking. It wasn't easy, but with the aid of nicotine gum and a lot of extra cookies, he'd finally cut his two-pack-a-day habit down to occasionally sneaking off to the basement for a cigarette.

The conversations I had with my grandfather were always pretty light and filled with tons of laughter. He had the best sense of humor of anyone I ever met. We lived a couple of hours apart from each other, but between visits, we'd talk on the phone and place our bets on sporting events—which would earn the winner weekly bragging rights and a cash prize of a whopping five dollars. But on this particular day, Gramp had a serious tone in his voice and three questions he wanted to ask me.

He began with: "Mike, do you think there's a God?" Instantly, I began to think, *Oh no . . . he's starting to really think about death now.* He once told me that he didn't like organized religion and felt it was better to be spiritual, but we'd never actually delved too deeply into this specific topic.

After pausing for a few seconds, I answered: "Yeah, Gramp. I definitely feel that there's a loving energy that runs through us and all of life. I don't think it's a judgmental, angry father figure in the sky, but I do believe in a source of love that sustains us and keeps the universe in order."

There was silence for a moment until he eventually spoke: "Yes, I guess I agree with that."

Next came the second question. "Mike, do you think there's a heaven?" Again, it was as if he were prepping himself for his earthly demise.

"Well," I replied, "I don't really envision the traditional pearly white gates and golden-harps scene, but I do believe that we'll transition from this world into a more loving and peaceful place—one where we may even be able to get a fresh opportunity to move on to another life."

Shortly after my answer, he again concurred with me. "Yes, I can see that, too."

And finally, the third one, which he'd been building up to in this philosophical conversation. I had no idea what to expect, but I knew it must be big. After one final pause, he was ready to ask me life's big question: "Well, Mike, if there's a heaven, and if there's a God . . . do you think he'd put a smoking section there for me?"

And there it was. Classic Moppy. Bursting into laughter, I responded, "You know, Gramp, I think, spiritually speaking, 'the smoking section' is what they refer to as *hell,* and I'm not sure that's where you want to be!"

Without hesitation, he came back with an answer that would reveal the very essence of his life. "That's all right," he said. "I can get along with anybody."

My grandfather's answer made me understand exactly why he had scores of friends and was loved by all. He *did* get along with everybody.

It also inspired me to conduct a heart-to-heart interview with him just before he died. I'll forever cherish the evening we spent sitting at his kitchen table talking about his Navy experiences, how he'd met my grandmother, his years working for the railroad, and the tremendous amount of success he'd achieved despite having only an eighth-grade education. If there was ever anyone who could tell a good story (or make you laugh hysterically), it was my grandfather.

After hours of reflecting upon the ups and downs of his 80 years, I finally had to ask him the big question: "Gramp, what do you think is the biggest reason you've had such a good life and, especially, so many friends?"

He paused, looked down at his coffee cup, and uncharacteristically gave me an answer with no joke or punch line attached to it: "I don't know, Mike. I guess . . . I just love everyone."

To me, the last two words in that sentence are stronger than anything I've written in this book. Envision our world if we collectively lived according to my grandfather's wisdom and *loved everyone*.

Imagine what would happen if every leader, politician, bank teller, waiter, teacher, CEO, woman, man, and child performed at least one sincere, loving act each day. This, I believe, is the pathway to both personal and global harmony. Simply by reconnecting to our true nature and using the power of kindness, we invite life to supply us with infinite opportunities to fulfill our own desires, while also creating a more loving and compassionate world.

What's more, you may just find yourself waking up one day with a whole new outlook on life . . . and the irresistible urge to "love everyone."

• • • • • •

Acknowledgments

This book and The Kindness Center simply would not exist if it weren't for the support of my loving family and friends. The first person I have to thank is my wonderful wife, Cara. Without your love and infinite patience as I've tried to "change the world," I'd be completely lost. Thank you for always encouraging me to follow my dreams—I love you so much. Thank you to . . .

. . . my son, Alex, for always listening to my long-winded philosophies on life; I am so proud of you.

. . . my mother, Patty Harnden, for being my biggest cheerleader. You and your positive energy are astonishing. Your ability to always see the good in people, circumstances, and the world is such an inspiration to me.

. . . Mike Hallahan, for all of your love and support over the years. You are truly a spiritual brother.

. . . my sister, Lisa Hallahan, for your gift of turning tears of sadness into tears of joy and uncontrollable laughter.

. . . my cousin Tammi Reynolds. You mean the world to me.

. . . my friend John Laverriere, for your creative input and huge heart.

. . . Reverend Jan Hryniewicz and the incredible people at Union Church in Biddeford Pool. I am overwhelmed by your never-ending kindness and generosity. Thank you!

I'd also like to thank two wonderful teachers, Tom Sferes and Diana Mullins, for your endless work in helping me create programs that promote kindness in schools. And to all of the students who treat me like a rock star when I walk through the school halls, you guys are the ones who truly rock!

To my amazing friend Marie . . . how could I ever begin to thank you? This book went from *local* to *global* because of you! Your friendship and *incredible* acts of kindness have changed my life forever. With all my heart, thank you.

My dear friend and editor, October Craig, thank you for helping my dream of sharing this book with the world come true. Our journey together has been pure magic. Between the hundreds of e-mails, dozens of phone calls, and you staying up *way* too late each night, we've truly created a gem of a book. You are proof that angels really do exist, and I cannot wait for our next project together. . . .

To my new family at Hay House: You all truly practice what you publish. Each and every one of you exudes love and positive energy. A special thanks to Patrick Gabrysiak and Jill Kramer—I am so grateful for your creative input, patience, and friendship. Just when I thought this book couldn't get any better, your spot-on suggestions took it to another level. Also, Reid Tracy, wow, isn't it amazing how one simple choice can change a guy's life?! Thank you for believing in me, this book . . . and for making my dream of becoming a Hay House author come true.

And finally, to the loving, divine energy that flows through my life every single day . . . thank you for choosing me to do this work. I've never felt more guided and loved since beginning this path of *living* kindness.

• • •   • • •

About the Author

Affectionately known as The Kindness Guy, **Michael J. Chase** is an author, inspirational speaker, and powerful voice for creating a kinder world. At the age of 37, following a life-changing epiphany, Michael ended an award-winning photography career to found The Kindness Center. After gaining extensive media attention for his 24 Hours of Kindness event, he quickly became a sought-after speaker and workshop leader throughout the world.

Considered an expert on the subject of kindness, Michael has inspired thousands to make positive choices that not only impact their own lives, but also those of others. Along with his loving wife and son, he currently lives in southern Maine. You can visit Michael's website at: **www.thekindnesscenter.com**.

• • • • • •

We hope you enjoyed this Hay House book. If you'd like to receive our online catalog featuring additional information on Hay House books and products, or if you'd like to find out more about the Hay Foundation, please contact:

Hay House, Inc., P.O. Box 5100, Carlsbad, CA 92018-5100
(760) 431-7695 or (800) 654-5126
(760) 431-6948 (fax) or (800) 650-5115 (fax)
www.hayhouse.com® • **www.hayfoundation.org**

• • •

Published and distributed in Australia by:
Hay House Australia Pty. Ltd., 18/36 Ralph St., Alexandria NSW 2015
Phone: 612-9669-4299 • *Fax:* 612-9669-4144 • www.hayhouse.com.au

Published and distributed in the United Kingdom by:
Hay House UK, Ltd., 292B Kensal Rd., London W10 5BE
Phone: 44-20-8962-1230 • *Fax:* 44-20-8962-1239 • www.hayhouse.co.uk

Published and distributed in the Republic of South Africa by:
Hay House SA (Pty), Ltd., P.O. Box 990, Witkoppen 2068
Phone/Fax: 27-11-467-8904 • www.hayhouse.co.za

Published in India by:
Hay House Publishers India, Muskaan Complex, Plot No. 3, B-2,
Vasant Kunj, New Delhi 110 070 • *Phone:* 91-11-4176-1620
Fax: 91-11-4176-1630 • www.hayhouse.co.in

Distributed in Canada by:
Raincoast, 9050 Shaughnessy St., Vancouver, B.C. V6P 6E5
Phone: (604) 323-7100 • *Fax:* (604) 323-2600 • www.raincoast.com

• • •

Take Your Soul on a Vacation

Visit **www.HealYourLife.com®** to regroup, recharge,
and reconnect with your own magnificence.
Featuring blogs, mind-body-spirit news, and life-changing
wisdom from Louise Hay and friends.

Visit **www.HealYourLife.com** today!